CW00493281

From Crimea to Olympic Bronze

ANNA RIZATDINOVA

FROM CRIMEA TO OLYMPIC BRONZE

Copyright © 2023 Anna Rizatdinova

All rights reserved. No part of this book may be
reproduced, or stored in a retrieval system, or transmitted
in any form or by any means, electronic, mechanical,
photocopying, recording, or otherwise, without express
written permission of the publisher.

ISBN: 9798397783569

DEDICATION

It is my pleasure to express sincere gratitude to my parents and to all those who made an invaluable contribution to my growth and helped and inspired me to discover life and to achieve more: Albina Deriugina, Serhii Bubka, Volodymyr Brynzak, Nina Umanets, Olena Govorova, Iryna Deriugina, Ireesha Blohina, Maryna Kardash, Svitlana Yevenko, Yuliia Atrushkevych, Lidia Vynogradna, Nataliia Yeromina, Nina Yeresko, Viktoriia Pinchuk, Oksana Babicheva, Alla Tykhonenko, Liudmyla Butkovskaia, Liudmyla Kuzmychova, Olha Melnytska, Anatolii Dumanov, Valentyna Synetska, Igor Oleksenko, Kostia Markitanov, Oleh Honcharenko, Narine Holubovych, Iryna Klymenko, Viacheslav Haran, Inesa Gruzynova, Olena Kolesnikova, Zina Zabeida and Oleh Zhezhel.

CONTENTS

PROLOGUE

I came up with the idea of writing a memoir in 2015, a year before the Olympic Games in Brazil. But then, I ran out of patience and had no more energy to make tremendous physical and mental efforts to win an Olympic medal.

Back then, I worked out at full stretch to prepare for the most critical moment of my life, the 2016 Summer Olympic Games in Rio de Janeiro. To cut the tension, I told my parents, "When it all ends, I'll write a book that may become a motivation for girls like me who once allowed themselves to dream big." But, of course, I didn't mean it then.

On August 21, 2016, I became the Olympic Games bronze medalist. After the triumph, the media limelight ceased, and I was finally left alone. So a year after I finished my professional gymnastics career, I made a real 180-degree change in my life. Now I am grateful to look back and share things I went through on the road to success.

I want to talk about the first uncertain steps in Rhythmic Gymnastics and the choreographers who helped me make those steps. I want to share the details of the rhythmic gymnast's life, which consists of routine hours-long everyday training and total self-control; the importance of finding the right coach who would believe in you, become your friend and a wise mentor, become the strictest judge, and simultaneously, your inspiration. Finally, I want to talk about the moments that may stress young athletes, about the acquired skill of not concentrating too much on the subjective judges' opinions.

Now I know that something that seems unfair at first can work for your benefit if you are on good terms with yourself and your work. There is a reason people say that there are no coincidences in sports; there are consequences.

I want to highlight the importance of finding the motivation to continue moving to the initial goal even after painful life lessons and failures. I want to tell you how vital it is to scream about the overwhelming emotions that rage inside you before the critical start, about the immense inner analysis, invisible even to the closest people, eventually leading to a result. A significant victory is a victory over yourself.

Sharing the details of successful performances at the World and European Championships and Olympic Games, which required complete devotion, titanic tension, and exhausting years-long work, made me proud and happy to be among the strongest athletes. This feeling is beyond comparison.

I want to laugh at funny incidents that happen in sports. The good news is now I can think about the past with no regrets. I also know that one shouldn't fear letdowns because they may eventually become a springboard for a new takeoff.

And above all, I want to share the innermost thought confirmed by years-long experience: under no circumstances may you give up on yourself or lose faith in yourself and the talent given by God. I am a firm believer that He blesses us all.

CHAPTER 1

TAKING THE FIRST STEP

The first thing I remember was the sea, as I was born in 1993 in Simferopol, Crimea. One of my brightest memories: I was around three years old, standing on the seashore, watching a ship sailing far away and eventually disappearing. There were no well-defined boundaries where the sea ended and the skies began. I couldn't stop thinking about what there was beyond the horizon. A combination of raging nature, a sense of balance, and tranquility lives in people born by the sea. It lives in me, too.

Every person has a spiritual place. Mine is Crimea, with its sparkling Black Sea, mighty mountains, symmetrical cypresses, fertile vineyards, the smell of juniper, and, indeed, the sun! It has been charging me with positive energy ever since I can remember. Memories of home and the Black Sea always helped me in big competitions.

I have always thought that Crimeans are radiant, happy people because they live in a paradise with many sunny days, and it's always warm there. The place where we are born also determines our destiny and our surroundings.

Figure 1. I belong to the sea.

The most important people for anyone are parents. I am fortunate. My parents always were my Mentors and Guardian Angels, and they still are.

My Mother, Oksana Rizatdinova, has the title of Master of Sport in Rhythmic Gymnastics; she is the honored coach of Ukraine and the Chief Coach in Rhythmic Gymnastics of the Autonomous Republic of Crimea. My Father, Serhii Rizatdinov, is a professional swimmer and a sea captain. If my Mom wasn't a coach, my life could have worked out differently. Now it's almost impossible to imagine.

Figure 2. Newborn Annie with Mom and Dad. July 16th, 1993

Since being in my Mom's womb, I have been in sports, which couldn't stay unnoticed. Being nine months pregnant, my Mother didn't want to take time off for maternity leave and continued coaching, so my fetal development was practically in the gym.

In 1993 Mom coached the Crimean Rhythmic Gymnastics Team to compete in an athletic contest in Zaporizhzhia. After training, she sent young gymnasts to the competition, and to avoid risks, she stayed home. I was born a week later – perhaps already a gymnast!

I recall one funny situation that brings up a smile in my family – my first performance in my long rhythmic gymnastics journey. In 1996 my Mom, with the girls' team and their head coach Liubov Serebrianska went to the training camp in Mykolaivka. I was three. My Dad was away on a work trip, and my Mom had to take me with her. But, of course, she was afraid that the presence of a child on a training ground could be distracting.

She was right. The sound of music from an old tape recorder signaled a coming 'catastrophe.' In no time, I rushed to the wooden bridge and started dancing, wearing only swimwear and a pair of flip-flops.

When somebody tried to stop me, I went dramatic. I couldn't sit still and watch how the athlete girls danced with ribbons and clubs. I had to do it too! So I gave them performances in Mykolaivka for a few days and earned my loyal crowd. Finally, on the third day, Liubov Yevseivna told my Mom that she appreciated the young Rizatdinova's genuine interest in sports. Still, I was constantly occupying the training area, and the management kindly asked my Mom to send me home to Simferopol.

So, I was on the way back home. I was crying and yelling in desperation. But there were no chances to stop the raging competitive nature inside me!

Before I turned five, we used to live in a dormitory of a sports boarding school. While my parents were saving up for their condo, Liubov Serebrianska, the head coach of the Crimean Rhythmic Gymnastics team, helped them. The dormitory was in the same building as the gym. So I only had to go downstairs to enter an appealing world of harmony, music, and dance. How magical was it for a little girl like me!

When I turned four, Mom tried to introduce me to Rhythmic Gymnastics. I wasn't excited about that because coaches immediately started to stretch me. There are children with that unique natural ability to do the split on the first try. Unfortunately, I wasn't one of them.

I lacked natural flexibility, so it was torture. Mom noticed my discontent but didn't try to persuade me to stay. So Rhythmic Gymnastics was on hold for us for a whole year.

However, I suffered from bow-leggedness. My Mom told me a story from when I was tiny, and we were going somewhere on a bus. A couple of women near us whispered to each other, "What a beautiful girl she is, but look at her legs!". That was the truth. My parents tried hard to help me. I had massage therapy and other daily treatments to amend the congenital disability. Step by step, the legs were straightening, but it was still far from perfect. Choosing Rhythmic Gymnastics as a sport, where every inch of your figure has to be perfect, with such legs already, was a significant challenge!

When I turned five, I asked my Mom to take me back to gymnastics. And that is how my professional career began. Nobody promised me a bright future; quite the opposite because Rhythmic Gymnastics required perfect physical characteristics. However, I didn't realize then how many serious obstacles I'd encounter on my way to success. It wasn't my concern, and attending training with other children was astonishing.

I remember my first leotards. Mom brought them from the Rhythmic Gymnastics World Championship in Japan. The first was pink with black welting, and the other was black with pink. They were so pretty that I wore them in the gym and at home. I even didn't realize at first that Rhythmic Gymnastics is a sport. I adored dancing and could do it at home for hours. My parents had a tape recorder, which was always on. Since Rhythmic Gymnastics relates to dancing and ballet, I used the music to inspire my perspective training.

Of course, my family encouraged me not only through music. My uncle made a stick of a wooden container, and my auntie attached an atlas ribbon cut from one of her accessories to it. Liubov Yevseivna Serebrianska gave me a ball and clubs as a gift. They were my first gymnastics apparatus. After that, I liked to scamper around a flat back and forth, imagining myself being an adult professional gymnast.

Figure 3. My first competition in Crimea

CHAPTER 2

HOW I DIDN'T BECOME A BALLERINA

I have loved dancing since childhood. As soon as the music started playing, the hidden engine inside me forced my body to move in tact and rhythm. Of course, the movements were often spontaneous, but I could dance for hours.

Michael Jackson became my music idol. What a significant number of choreography routines to his songs was created by me at home! His music videos have many impressive dance movements, so I often tried to copy them but added some of my own: a couple of signature dance steps, combinations, and leaps. I was my choreographer and director. I was my own Star.

According to my parents, my artistic talent was fiercely breaking out. However, Dad constantly reiterated, "Sweetheart, you have a sense of rhythm and charisma." At the time, I didn't know the meaning of the word 'charisma,' but Dad made it sound mysterious and intriguing.

Later, professional coaches and choreographers admitted my subtle perception of music, rhythm, and dramatic facial expressions. In particular, I was graded higher for these traits than other gymnasts in the sports competitions. But the first one who noticed my dance talent was my music teacher in kindergarten.

Already a little gymnast, I was still attending kindergarten. A lovely lady Iryna taught dance and music. She adored me and noticed my talent in the first lessons. I understand now why. At the age of five, I could do splits and bridges, and the most impressive part was that the sound of music immediately sparked me to start dancing.

I quickly became a leading lady of performance in kindergarten. Even though two other girls were taking ballroom dance classes, I was honored to perform solo, not them. Knowing what I'm capable of, Iryna designed dramatic dance parts just for me.

The most memorable one was "Carmen." I was six years old, performing on the stage of the vast hall of Simferopol Medical Institute. I was in a black dress and a pair of velvet shoes, the skirt and the sleeves decorated with red double ruching. I had castanets in my hands and a red flower in my hair.

As soon as the first chords of famous Georges Bizet's opera sounded out, I started to move with the music. The castanets were creating the rhythmic chattering. A vibrant dance began. Then the music took me with its flow. It was my first actual performance in front of an adult audience. Spectators were charmed! After the performance, they burst into thunderous applause. I was on cloud nine.

It is so impressive how our fate sometimes knits its lace repeating the pattern: in 15 years, in Turkey, in the 2014 Izmir Rhythmic Gymnastics World Championship, my performance was accompanied by the same music. Then I got a bronze medal for ribbon exercises accompanied by Carmen. I'll tell you about this precious experience a little bit later. It deserves a separate chapter.

Back then, my kindergarten music teacher Iryna was proud of me. She saw a natural Spanish dancer in me. And it wasn't surprising as Iryna had been dancing herself and studying at The Moscow Vocational School of Choreography. She often invited her peers to Crimea. They were discussing the opening nights in the theatre, classical ballet performances, and arguing about the leading actresses of The Bolshoi and The Kirov Theatres. Once when they came, they started to talk about gifted children. She used it as a chance to show them the video of my performance.

After watching my dance, Volodymyr Vasiliev said, "This girl feels the rhythm very well and is artistically sensitive."

"She has to move to Moscow and study at Bolshoi Ballet Academy. Then, one day, she might even perform at Bolshoi Theatre."

Back then, Russia and Ukraine were friendly, so Iryna told my parents, adding that she had the same opinion. She thought my talent had to progress. Mom and Dad were thinking about Vasiliev's offer for the whole spring. But they couldn't imagine sending their only child to study far away from home. And this is how I didn't become a ballerina.

CHAPTER 3

TIME TO TAKE IT SERIOUSLY

Once I got older, the time for fun, laid-back dances was over. Carefully rewatching the recordings of my exercises, Mom considered my skills weak for professional Rhythmic Gymnastics. Unfortunately, nature did not give me much to work with to build a successful sports career. And yet I was eager to train. The only thing I possessed was dedication. And we decided to give it a try.

I was in love with this sport! There may have been something profound within myself that didn't let me give up. I fancied working with apparatus, loved catching a ball, rotating a hoop, and performing on a floor to various music, particularly Michael Jackson's songs.

But immediately after the start of intensive training, I stepped back. Again, I needed more natural flexibility and stretching skills; my arches needed to be higher. These were the facts, and they were evident to me, my parents, and my coaches.

Mom and Dad tried to ensure I had to exert myself more to see the result. I constantly heard from my Dad, "If you work hard, sooner or later, you will succeed." But, he would also say: "You lack flexibility. So, let's put more effort into it."

Splits and bridges are exercises taught to children aged five or six. To do these exercises correctly, one is supposed to be flexible. It was a real problem for me. Physically, I often felt discomfort, like a

9

nagging pain, etc. I could do the exercises, but the classes didn't bring me joy anymore. We had to do something about it.

Stretching is a set of exercises to extend the body's range of motion: joints and muscles. In the very first stretching class, the coach made us do splits. For example, if it was a right front split, the right leg had to extend forward and the left one to the rear of the torso. And vice versa. Some gifted children could do all exercises excellently on the first try, but there were very few.

The main goal for the kid gymnasts was to do a split touching the floor. I couldn't do it. I had to ask for help. There were two options for how to improve stretching skills. The first one is in the gym. My body refused to loosen up muscles when coaches started actively pushing me in stretching. So, there was another option left. We made a tough decision at the family meeting: to work not only at the gym but at home, too. So was said – so was done.

Figure 4. Kherson. Visiting Grandma

After that, I started the next day with stretching exercises. Doing it in the morning after sleep was vital while muscles were still relaxed, inactive, soft, and not warmed up. There I remember two chairs brought into my room. The right leg was on the front chair, and the left was on the back. The task was to loosen all muscles to the maximum and under the body's weight to get closer to the floor. I kept myself in that position for about ten minutes for the right leg and almost the same time for the left.

You would have sympathized with me if you knew how painful it was to stretch the front and back muscles simultaneously. But I achieved the result. Gradually, the amplitude of muscle stretch increased. The process was quite painful but efficient.

I think that I acquired a strong-willed personality right in that period. Any child's main difficulty is repeating the same challenging and often painful exercises. You don't understand why you need it when you are five or six. Routine tasks can be complex even for adults; restless and curious children, in their turn, often hunger for something new, unknown, and exciting. And what is new and interesting about two annoying chairs in front of you every morning? How not to start being down in the dumps? At those very moments, my parents were there for me.

Figure 5. Kherson. My first public performance

They patiently explained that all my efforts weren't in vain, proving that I was doing an important thing that would be useful in the future. It encouraged me. I believed my parents.

11

Thankfully, I wasn't a naughty child; I exercised every day for months and years. As a result, my stretching skills improved, and my muscles became softer and softer. Finally, my parents and I overcame the first big challenge so I could move forward.

CHAPTER 4

DADDY'S GIRL

I want to devote a whole chapter to my Father, who significantly shaped my personality. My Father is a very deliberate, rigorous, and disciplined man. On top of that, he is active, goal-oriented, and very hard-working. Labor is a vital part of his life. He is truly self-made.

When he was a teenager, and later during his studies at the Vocational Military School, he used to go swimming and later pursued it professionally. He hates laziness. Later, when he worked as a sea captain and if he noticed a lazy guy on the ship, he immediately sent him back to the shore, regardless of position or rank. So naturally, it affected the bringing-up system of his only daughter.

Mom and Dad were teaching me to be independent. At kindergarten, I could dress and put off clothes without making a scene and tie shoes alone. My parents always treated me like an adult. I wasn't raised spoiled. They were strict but supportive friends. If I couldn't understand something, they patiently explained it until I got it. We could talk for hours.

My Dad and I had our ritual. Almost every Sunday, when Dad was home, we would go to the puppet theatre or circus together. After I turned five, Dad would buy only one theatre ticket, and that ticket was for me. Dad wanted me to mature. He accompanied me to the theatre building. We would say goodbye at the stairs, and then, feeling like an adult, I was marching ahead the corridor to the show, holding a ticket in my hands.

My Father was proud of my behavior as it was rare for a child at that age to be so independent. He constantly emphasized it and praised me.

Dad often made firm decisions. I clearly remember what happened to me in kindergarten once. He came early afternoon to take me to the training but saw a crowd of children in the playroom. There were big boxes and bags in the middle of the room. Every child could take something they liked. All boys and girls were smiling and playing with building blocks, dolls, and cars. Everyone was happy. I rushed to my Dad with sparkles in my eyes and begged, "Daddy, we've got a new toy delivery; we've been waiting for it for so long. May I stay here until the evening and skip gymnastics training? Please!"

He could see how fascinated the children were with the unpacking and how much I didn't want to leave. He began to doubt, but not for long. Finally, he took me aside and said, "Annie, every person has a choice. One may spend childhood hanging around, sitting on the bench, talking about nothing, nibbling sunflower seeds, and playing in the yard, but later would not have the opportunity to obtain the benefits of our wonderful world. But if you work while others relax, in the future, you will enjoy the results."

Those words didn't change my opinion. And Dad used a trick. First, he sugar-coated the upcoming training, telling me it would be as memorable as my excitement with new toys in kindergarten. Then, finally, he talked me into it. And therefore, giving up the toys, I agreed with Dad and chose to work in the gym. He was satisfied. When we came to the gym, he froze and said to me, looking straight into my eyes, "The ability to say no to yourself is a victory. I am very proud of you."

We had a special bond. We were best friends. I always knew: whatever might happen to me, he would always be on my side and protect me. Later he proved it a thousand times. Also, the optimistic attitude to life shared by both of us bound us even more.

Once, my classmates and I, accompanied by a school teacher, went on a one-day bus excursion around Crimea during the school holidays. As usual, Dad came to say goodbye.

The trip started with a children's laugh and a lot of fun. But it wasn't so funny on the way home. Even now, Dad often recalls the episode. The bus parked in the city center, next to a café. The door opened. Children were getting off the bus in absolute silence, exhausted, sleepy, and some on the edge of crying. Who knows, maybe they were tired, perhaps they missed their parents. Dad started worrying about what happened on the trip to his precious daughter.

Suddenly, upbeat and cheerful, I jumped out of the bus. I was the only one smiling. Those parents who felt sorry for their children and even started criticizing teachers for an exhausting excursion stood still, surprised, and watched my Dad and me happily going home.

Dad was always very strict with himself and with others. I remember a summer camp in Alushta, Crimea, at the Spartak Olympic Center in 2009. Exhausted gymnasts ran their last circles around the stadium on that tiring day. Mom and Dad were standing aside and talking, sneakily watching the runners. All girls from the Ukrainian National Rhythmic Gymnastics Team ran perfectly well; their speed and technique were great.

My Dad wanted me to run as well as the girls do. However, he thought I needed to be better at running. Dad was an excellent runner at school and wanted me to have the same skills. He had a great power of persuasion and convinced me to run. Later, I figured that Albina Deriugina always admitted that running was the basis of good physical condition.

My Dad always kept his promises. So was said – so was done. We started to run. When we finally bought our condo, its location was perfect for a walk through the park to the gym.

But we were not walking; we were running along the river Salhyr, along the tennis club, and stopped only at the sports complex "Dynamo," where I had my training. Soon enough, Dad could watch me run, and his eyes flashed with genuine pride. But, of course, nobody forced me to do it; I just wanted to be the best in everything, which made him proud.

After many years, I was one of the best runners on our National Team. When I moved to Kyiv, I used to run around the stadium and along the Livoberezhna Quay, where I bought my condo later.

After a while, I realized I wasn't running only for my Dad; at the end of the day, it was all for me and my future. Dad was happy feeling his input into my strong character, especially when I ran in late autumn and winter. I remember how much I didn't want to run because afterward, there were two more pieces of training. Generally speaking, the tricky thing is to overcome yourself and your laziness. So I didn't consider it to be a victory at first.

Frankly, I learned to enjoy running. It was so cool to come to the training having a red nose after a winter jog. Everyone was still sleepy but me. I was full of energy and ready to work. After all, Dad taught me well.

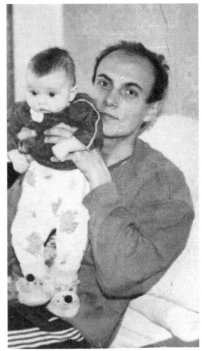

Figure 6. Dad and his Daddy's girl

16

CHAPTER 5

MODIFIED CHOREOGRAPHY, OR PRICELESS LESSONS

Rhythmic Gymnastics has a lot in common with dance and choreography. It was brought to the world by American dancer Isadora Duncan. After being dissatisfied with classical ballet, she introduced a new contemporary revolutionary dance form. She created the 'free dance' style, where artistic expression and flow collide with old-fashioned technique.

She is believed to be the inventor of rhythmic gymnastics. Her famous scarf was a great-grandfather of what people know now as apparatus. Rumor has it that the scarf gradually got replaced by ribbon. In this way, our sport became a mixture of art and dance.

I was fortunate to have a great choreography teacher. Nina Bahautdinova was a former ballerina; she performed on the most famous stages, such as the Crimean State Opera and Ballet Theatre. She used to be a real, local celebrity. We had a special bond with her. She was more than a teacher to me; she was my godmother.

She coached a couple of ballroom dancers and came to teach us only a few times a week. And as far as I'm concerned, she chose the Simferopol Rhythmic Gymnastics school as a principal place of work just because of me. So, Nina played a crucial role in my life. Although she was my godmother, she would never go easy on me. On the contrary, I always had higher requirements than others.

Traditionally, choreography for gymnastics is classical ballet warm-up, where the girls stand beside a ballet bar and perform particular movements. Nina used her method; she taught us 'modified' choreography.

For a whole lesson, an hour and a half, we danced in the middle of the gymnastic carpet. The uniqueness of the method lay in performing the set of movements - plié, pas tendu, grandpas jeté, rond de jambe par terre, adagio – supporting all body weight on the tips of fully extended feet and without holding on to a ballet bar. That way, we worked on body alignment and balance. Furthermore, we didn't touch the ground with our heels at all. It was unusual for the time and even seemed to contradict the laws of physics.

After the lesson, we worked on pirouettes. First, we held still all pirouettes' forms for one minute each. Then we kept spinning all types of pirouettes for half an hour. There was no chance to skip. The dance teacher would never let you go home.

Nina was so gifted. She would always notice every tiny body move. Nina could find the right words and tips for every gymnast. She was trying to find an individual approach for every girl. And every time, she managed to find it. So, there was a good reason why Crimean gymnasts always performed grand pirouettes. We all were not willing to disappoint Nina.

Later, in Kyiv, I realized how difficult it is to work without an insightful choreographer. Sometimes, when I returned home after the competitions, my body balance worsened because of fatigue. If Nina had been there, she would say, "Put this shoulder forward, turn this leg out more, pull the shoulder blade to the knee," after I would perform a perfect pirouette. But without her, I would spend hours restoring balance.

All the time, Nina tried to help me succeed and cared about me. When all the girls would go on the break, relax after the training, chat with each other, and laugh, I would stay in the gym, and Nina would work on improving my feet arches. I would sit in front of her. First, she would take my feet and push the insteps with her hands pulling them down. We would spend fifteen minutes on it every day for three years.

Eventually, I got really 'nice feet.' But it wasn't easy. Sometimes I wanted to rush to the changing room with others, hang out with the girls, and finally relax before working on apparatus, but I would remain at the gym to improve my feet arches. Then, we would devote fifteen more minutes to pirouettes to improve the balance.

A well-developed pirouette with an outstanding balance is one of the essential skills necessary for ballet dancers and gymnasts. So soon after, pirouettes became crucial and the best-performed elements of my program.

If you ask a foreigner to tell the first thing that comes to mind when you mention my name, almost all would say, "Rizatdinova is about pirouettes."

Many thought that I had the talent to do many complicated pirouettes at a time. Naturally, it was an acquired skill. Nina and I worked on pirouettes every single day for years. Later I could link and mix different types of spins in one; I could change two or three leg positions or the position of a torso while doing a spin. It became my signature in Rhythmic Gymnastics, and judges always graded me high. There are some elements that nobody repeated until today. The pirouettes also helped me to win my Olympic medal.

Thinking back, sometimes I can't understand how I could do it all at the age of six. For twenty minutes each morning, I stretched and went to do choreography. Then, after the choreography training, I would focus on improving feet arches, then fifteen more minutes for balance and pirouettes. And only after I used to go to my second training. It was like in the fairy tale about Cinderella, with no minute to waste. It was challenging for a child.

Of course, nobody prohibited other girls from training more, but for some reason, I was the one who did it consistently. Then, finally, diligence and regular training paid off. Gradually my legs started to straighten, and I became flexible enough and got a nice, high instep. When I turned ten, I almost looked like a real gymnast.

However, the sport wasn't the only thing in my life. Nina helped significantly in my spiritual growth. She was a deeply religious person and managed to inspire me, too. As a devoted godmother, Nina took me to the Holy Communion when I was five or six. She helped me to study Bible. I didn't realize the meaning of all this until I grew up. Nina showed me a different perspective. It's impossible to succeed in the sport without believing in the Divine, yourself, and your calling.

When I am on the verge of giving up, I refer to God and feel no shame in talking about it. I always had that special bond with the Lord throughout my sports career. I would ask Him to be on my side at difficult times, and before competitions, I would ask Him to help me to handle fear. And it always worked for me.

CHAPTER 6

HASTY DECISIONS

People sometimes do irrational things, make hasty decisions, and play senseless games that may lead to unintended consequences. We do this with good intentions, but later it leads to something terrible. It happened to me, too, when I was 13. And my Mom was already training me at the time.

There were precise rules at the Simferopol Rhythmic Gymnastics School. One of them included weight management.

Many people wonder why weight management is so vital for rhythmic gymnastics. There are a couple of reasons for that. First, our sport is all about aesthetics and performance. Complicated body elements look better when performed by someone tall and slender, especially on camera. Lately, gymnastics is all about performance. For instance, even rope is not used as much as an apparatus because it almost remains unnoticed on TV: it moves too fast.

But most importantly, weight management helps to prevent injuries. Gymnasts put a lot of pressure on their feet; this is just the specifics of our sport. For bones and joints to endure endless jumps and performing elements, the weight has to be proper. Usually, doctors from our National Team calculate the ideal weight for each gymnast.

However, the rules are loose in practice, and we tend to be extreme as children. For example, we were afraid to drink enough water for many years because water weight shows immediately and would lead to bloating. Of course, any dietician now would say avoiding water is wrong, but back when we trained, the Internet wasn't as accessible in Ukraine as it is now. We were just desperate kids, thriving for perfection and afraid to disappoint our coach.

Electronic Scales were our judges. Gymnasts checked their weight twice daily: in the morning before the first training and in the evening after the second. Coaches would track the morning's and evening's weight.

Sometimes those tiny numbers made our lives even more complicated. Extra pounds were punishable. Protests and a general feeling of resentment arose not only among the coaches but among the gymnasts as well. Nobody was living a calm and quiet life. Coaches would be angry with girls who gained some extra weight, and the girls, in their turn, would loathe and even call that familiar weighting procedure names. But, of course, no one organized an absolute riot. If you chose Rhythmic Gymnastics, you knew the deal. And it was a deal breaker if you wanted to treat yourself to something tasty.

However, we came up with a trick. Once in the evening, the girls were finishing up some exercises with my Mom. So two more girls and I went to the coach's office, where the scales were, our 'execution place.' At first, we weighed ourselves and then realized we were a little extra that day. I don't remember who was the one to come up with an excellent idea to cheat the scales, but we decided to act immediately. It was time to stop getting nervous about those extra pounds!

An act of sabotage took its place on Saturday. We were fully aware that the only day off was coming, and after it, all girls would put on a pound and a half, and the most undisciplined ones might gain up to two pounds, as they could allow themselves to eat more without doing any exercises. We often dreamed of attending the weight check without gaining extra weight. Then we would be praised, not punished. Monday, the day after the day off, is usually hard for gymnasts.

I can't recall who said, "There is a way to cheat everybody; we need to use a trick with scales." But we all supported the idea. We found a piece of paper and cut it into small pieces. One girl cut the paper with a utility knife, and the other watched for coaches in the doorway. And I was stuffing small amounts into the battery holder. Then we locked it and decided to recheck the weight with the help of our new electronic friend. I stepped on the scales, saw the numbers, and could not find words; there was half a pound less on the screen!

The first test worked well. Then, overjoyed, we cut up so much paper that we could hardly place all pieces into the holder. Then a miracle happened! The scales showed a result weightless of two pounds. So, happy and upbeat that we could eat plenty of food at the weekend, we went home sharing terrific news with other girls.

Monday began in a festive mood. Girls weighed themselves individually, but the weight was in order, and our coaches looked confused. Twenty-six girls went through weight checks without problems, but abruptly the scales froze, showing an error on the twenty-seventh girl. My Mom and two more coaches were in the room. Taking turns, they spun the scales and then started to shake them. At some point, I saw my Mom's hands on the bottom of the battery holder. She found out about our scam!

The papers were flying over the room. Cold shivers started to wrap my body up. I wanted to disappear, but it was impossible. A great scandal broke out at the school. Coaches knew that one of us did it. They rechecked our weight. Almost two pounds more for every girl! They started to look for a plotter and called everyone to enter the coaches' office. It was harsh.

All the girls knew I played a big part in the scam. Even though many girls were in the 'investigation room' before me, nobody ratted me out. Before questioning, older gymnasts said to younger ones, "Nobody should say anything about Annie."

But when it came to me, I gave up. I felt so ashamed; my cheeks and ears were red and hot. I started to cry and confessed. I took all the blame. Older girls were angry with me, "Why have you done that? All the group has undergone a tough procedure of questioning, and nobody has let you down".

There was a massive scandal. Mom decided to expel me from the sports school; she considered my actions humiliating and didn't allow me to stay. The verdict was like a gunshot, "Your Rhythmic Gymnastics classes are over. There is no place in sports for a liar!" Now I understand that Mom tried to give me a lesson, but as a child, I thought she was for real.

At home, I tried to talk to my Mom a hundred times and asked her to forgive me, but Mom's decision was unwavering. The tension between us was increasing day by day. It was so awful that we brought this situation home. Can you imagine how it feels when you stay with a person in the same room but do not communicate with each other at all? It was like torture.

Mom didn't answer me when I asked something, demonstrating that she did not want to talk to me. It was severe and brought me on the verge of losing patience. I was constantly crying. Once I finally lost patience, I knelt before my Mom and shouted, "Mom, forgive me, please! Could you take me to Rhythmic Gymnastics classes back?" But she didn't even miss a beat. Incredible self-control!

Dad was away sailing, so he couldn't help me. Two weeks have passed. Suddenly at night, when I was in bed, Mom came into my room. And I heard: "Training is tomorrow at nine." Then she left. I burst into tears. Then I couldn't fall asleep for a long time. There was no happier person in the whole world than me.

The following day I was met like a hero by gymnasts. I thought Mom had already turned the page, but she didn't! She ignored me. Music was on, and my exercise started, and Mom immediately looked away and went to work with other gymnasts. Mom's assistant, Veronika Belyaeva, took over. She was Mom's former student, a Master of Sports, and a world-class coach. She helped me during those difficult times and significantly contributed to my career. We often worked together.

Days went by. I went to the training every day. I worked hard, but the Crimean National Team head coach ignored me. I felt embarrassed, disappointed, and sad. I had yet to learn how long the situation would last. Mom finally forgave me only after two weeks. But the sorrow and regret were not leaving me for a long time. It was how I learned that lying is wrong.

After reading this chapter, gymnasts would want to avoid repeating my experience. So, it is better to refrain from cheating scales or doing other tricks. But the truth always comes out. And consequences of it may even make things worse. So, stand out against your weight in an honest way. I know your rival is strong. But I'm sure you have enough power to defeat it.

CHAPTER 7

PRIMARY EDUCATION

I attended school №40 with an in-depth study of Physics and Mathematics in Simferopol. My parents chose Mathematics only from a practical point of view: the gym was across the road from the school. All gymnasts avoided this school, considering its program too demanding, but after I started studying there, other girls came, too.

I had no problems with my studies in primary school. Our grade, 1st A in old Ukrainian traditions, was one of the top grades in the school. I was fortunate to have a great class teacher. Valentyna Pavlivna announced to our parents at the first meeting that their kids had to attend any after-school activity of their choice. She considered that every child should have a hobby or be involved in extracurricular activities. At that time, I was already deeply engaged in rhythmic gymnastics.

Valentyna Pavlivna became a significant person in my life. She highlighted my achievements, noticed my potential, and encouraged me to do sports. She also helped me to cope with a study program. She didn't care if I missed a school day because she could already notice my creativity mixed with workaholism. She also used to praise me a lot at the parents' meetings.

It was a great encouragement for my parents, who would spend all their money and put great effort into 'our collective purpose.' Valentyna Pavlivna showed the true wisdom of a teacher when I skipped lessons because of competitions; she would stay with me after classes and explain the missing topic so I would not fall behind my classmates.

Usually, in the first part of the day, I was studying. After that, I would go to do rhythmic gymnastics. At first, I attended one training a day and could easily catch up with my studies. I wouldn't say I liked maths; I had to force myself to do the studies. It caused a lot of difficulties, but Dad considered maths an essential subject, so he always helped me get the hang of it at home. Once, I even managed to get the highest possible grade for a test. There was a real celebration in my family. But it lasted only a short time, and no matter how much effort we put into it, maths wasn't my favorite subject.

However, I was good at the arts. Later, in secondary school, I liked geography and history. And in high school, I fell in love with biology, anatomy, and literature. I liked poetry. Learning poems by heart was easy for me, and I enjoyed reciting poems in class and at home. At secondary school, it became apparent that I was more into liberal arts.

I loved reading. There were many books on the history of civilizations, the history of different states, Crimea, and books about geographical discoveries. I would devour them one after another. Nevertheless, due to constant absence from the lessons because of competitions at secondary school, I got terrible grades in geography. My Dad was so angry that he went to school with me and asked the teacher to test me again in front of him. Of course, the teacher had to correct my grade. But, to tell you the truth, the teacher saw it as a relief when Dad added that I would switch to distance learning.

Not all people were as eager to help as my first teacher. Some teachers were mad at me because I often skipped their lessons. But I had to choose what was more important. For me, it was gymnastics.

I needed to understand what I was involved in. Even when I provided extraordinary documentary evidence issued by Simferopol Rhythmic Gymnastics School that allowed me to miss lessons, everyone still could not understand why Rizatdinova was constantly skipping classes. They felt jealous of me because they thought, "She's carefree, doesn't have to go to school." And when I came back to class after a long absence, I felt embarrassed.

My classmates displeasedly looked at me; I could see that on their faces. "Look, our dancer has finally shown up," they would say. That's why I didn't have friends at school. Once you start making friends, you leave for a week, and it's over.

Later, in high school, I noticed my relationship with boys was complicated. I didn't fall for anybody. Nobody helped me to carry my schoolbag home. Then, on Valentine's Day, there was a heart-shaped box in the class, and everyone could put Valentine's cards inside it. After that, the girls counted who got the most cards. I only got a few. They always liked somebody close, in front of their eyes, but not the one who was a bird of passage.

Figure 7. My first photoshoot

I was always 'lucky' to attend school right for some test. And, of course, I usually failed. Sometimes I tried to cheat, but it didn't work out properly. I couldn't do it; my red cheeks would betray me. So I had to retake the tests.

Every test was like a challenge and caused a lot of stress. I realized other children in the class knew more than me, which bothered me greatly. I remember we had to pass an annual maths test, and I was shaking like an aspen leaf. The one who wouldn't pass would have to retake it; if you failed again, you had to retake a whole year of classes. I was on the verge of losing consciousness from anxiety.

"How dare I let my smart parents down? What a shame it is for my family," I thought. Finally, I couldn't stand that anymore and shared my thoughts with my godmother. I told her about my fear, and she advised me to take a small icon to the test and put it on the desk in front of me. She said my worries would go away. I did what she said. And I passed the test!

My parents could notice that I loved rhythmic gymnastics; I had already achieved some success and became the best gymnast in Crimea. Unfortunately, at that time, I had a lot of trouble at school. In addition, I was often away for international competitions and had to skip the lessons; it took a lot of work to catch up with the program.

I was often anxious. I've got that type of personality: everything should be structured and explained in detail when I need to understand something. If I skip one topic, I need help understanding the next one. So, I got nervous because of that quite often. Exhausted after the training, I stayed at school after classes. The teachers would explain to me topics that needed to be clarified.

When sport becomes for you more than just a hobby, your priorities change. Gymnastics was my true calling, so I preferred it over academic studies.

CHAPTER 8

MOM AS A COACH AND HOW IT FEELS

There are always two sides to a coin. How would you feel if your Mother was a coach? How would you feel if she was coaching you? In Rhythmic Gymnastics, it's not uncommon. The most successful examples of such successions are Albina Deriugina and Iryna Deriugina, Kateryna Serebrianska and Liubov Serebrianska, Olena Vitrychenko and Nina Vitrychenko, Viktoria Bessonova and Anna Bessonova, Zhulieta Shishmanova and Kristina Guiourova, Silvia Miteva-Divcheva and Silvia Miteva and many more.

It was my burden, too. But, of course, this kind of cooperation has pros and cons. Sometimes, it may be challenging to separate work stuff from family matters. But those who manage to do it will succeed.

Since I was seven, I have performed in Crimean competitions. At the age of nine, I had already won Crimean and Simferopol championships and city tournaments. At that point, people in the industry started to gossip about my Mom being a head coach of Crimean

Figure 8. Yalta, Crimea. Mom and I

30

Simferopol Rhythmic Gymnastics School. People assumed my career was going somewhere only because of my Mom. I can clearly remember my reaction when I heard those fake news. I felt miserable and suffered from prejudice towards me.

I could hear it everywhere. People said, "Only because she is a trainer's daughter, she wins the competitions." So there was a period when I stopped believing in myself, thinking, what if I didn't deserve triumph? What if I succeeded only owing to my Mom's position? But I didn't share my feelings with anyone.

Mom's view on this subject was firm: being a trainer's daughter is about having doubled responsibility. First, I had to be far better than other gymnasts to avoid rumors and awkwardness. Second, I had to prove my championship by demonstrating great results, so I worked on it.

All of Simferopol Rhythmic Gymnastics School coaches trained me. I tried to always look up to each of them, taking helpful hints from all. Mom would never interfere in our training process.

The one thing she would always manage was costumes. All the ideas of my costumes since early childhood belonged to her. Only sometimes could she suggest music or a song and keep an eye on my stretching at home.

Mom didn't want me to join her team; she tried to delay that moment as much as possible. Later she explained her decision by giving the example of the tense relationships between Katia Serebrianska and Liubov Serebrianska. She didn't want to ruin our bond. When Mother and daughter communicate almost 24/7, that is not easy.

But the time came, and we faced a dilemma. I started to progress and needed Mom as a coach. Even Dad said, "Oksana, take Annie to your team; she needs you in her training now."

And I was accepted into my Mom's group. It was a leading team at the school. Mom's former student Veronika Belyaeva, a Master of Sports and a silver medalist of the European Championship in all-around group events, started coaching me. It happened before the Championship of Ukraine held in Dnipro. It was my first big competition at the national level, where I was performing on the same stage with gymnasts from the famous Deriugina School and gymnasts from the National Team.

A cold shiver ran down my spine if someone mentioned the school of the Deriuginas. First, I had to present myself well. Mom realized that. I needed to show a good jump; it was only possible to do so by having trained with the older, more experienced girls.

Time was not on our side, so Mom took the chance, and we trained very hard. My Mom and I both were very involved in what we were doing. I was the youngest in her team but still managed to get chosen for the competition. Nobody thought I would win; there were more experienced girls in the group born in 1992. A year makes a difference in our sport.

When the day came, I performed all the routines perfectly well and instantly became third at the Championship of Ukraine. Deriugina's gymnasts took first and second places. In my case, third place was an achievement. After that, people started treating me like a big gymnast.

Everyone realized that I wasn't just a coach's daughter but a genuine athlete. After that, experts started to pay closer attention to me, especially after I won the next championship in Kharkiv.

At the same time, attending Mom's Rhythmic Gymnastics group was challenging but exciting. I grew professionally by being with more experienced girls. Some of them were five or six years older than me. It inspired me not only to catch up with them but also to exceed them. I already got ambitions.

When I started training with Mom, we realized that dramatic expressions and emotions might become my specialty. For this reason, we would select music carefully, look for some film scenes or pieces of classical music, and search for a unified look. However, I was undoubtedly too young to perform such serious routines.

My young age did not give me excuses. I had competitions one after another. Then, I started to travel around the country and abroad. The movements of my body were balanced and refined. But Mom noticed all imperfections: a lack of stretching skills in some elements, not perfect feet, or a bad jump. And we worked non-stop.

After working with Serebrianska for a long time and absorbing the coaching experience of the Deriugins, Mom was fully aware of the proper preparation for serious competition. The preparation model of the National Team was fundamental for us. Mom immediately brought new techniques to Crimea.

I demonstrated consistent results, won competitions, and gradually enhanced my skills. At some point, our relationship with Mom became complicated. For sixteen hours every day, we talked only about rhythmic gymnastics. Then, we returned home after the training, and over dinner, we discussed what I had done well, what needed improvement, and what and how I should improve. Then, when I went to bed, Mom bent down to kiss me and gave me tips for the following training day.

Sometimes it annoyed me. I wanted somebody to sympathize with me after a hard day. At that time, I didn't have a Mother-Mother anymore; I had a Mother-Coach. So, naturally, she praised me quite often and encouraged my good performance. But as a teenager, I needed different things. We didn't talk about movies, fashion, boys, or friends: We only talked about sports.

It's hard to describe your feelings when you come to the gym and see Mom right before you, but you must treat her as a coach. And all the time, she requires you to do more. You have to do everything flawlessly. And along with that, you get one more responsibility not to disappoint your Coach and your Mom. This double duty was tiring.

And again, weight management. My diet was not strictly limiting. Mom handled it smartly: she cooked breakfast, lunch, and dinner. Usually, sweets and Rhythmic Gymnastics are our worst enemies, so there never were any cakes, candies, or buns on our table. But at the same time, we could go to the café on the weekend, and Mom would let me eat one tiny slice of dessert.

Her goal was to teach me how to manage my weight by myself. When I put on even a little weight, I faced a difficult and unpleasant conversation at home.

Mom would always worry for me a lot at the competitions. She never watched my performances at Ukrainian Championships. Usually, she was one of the judges, though she didn't glance at me even once. You could ask how then she graded me. After my performance, she asked the judge next to her how well I performed and how clean my elements were. And based on the answer, she would give me an average grade.

She was so nervous that she couldn't raise her eyes. It continued even when I became the best gymnast on the National Team. I often begged her to watch my performance, and she would say yes many times. But she couldn't do it.

In 2008, when I turned fifteen, working together became harder and harder. I remember having a terrible fight in the last training before a competition. I was so messy that day. Mom was too nervous and criticized me a lot.

Finally, she stung me, saying, "Your Dad is sailing; he is always away from home and earning money for your leotards and music. Do you even know how much it costs? I work with you from morning till night, but you cannot pull your socks up and do anything well!"

It was like a stab in the heart. Things got too personal. It looked like everyone in our family was working hard, sacrificing everything for me, but I didn't meet their expectations. So, what were all those efforts for?

After that conversation, I thought a lot. I wish to move to Kyiv to train at 'The Deriugina School.' I realized our relationship with Mom was worse than before. I had to leave a Mother-Coach to keep a Mother-Friend, or I risked losing both.

Shortly after, I told her about my decision. Then, finally, we both could understand that it was time to separate. I had to go; Mom had to let me go. And after half a year, I left for Kyiv.

CHAPTER 9

IF YOUR CHILD WANTS TO BE A GYMNAST

In this chapter, I would like to discuss the parent's role in raising a future athlete. Over the years, I watched many parents bring their children to the gymnastics class. Unfortunately, a lot of them made similar mistakes.

Some parents, choosing a sport for their child, are often driven by their ambitions and broken dreams. But they also don't consider what their little one wants. Unfortunately, it happens a lot in our sport.

Of course, it can be difficult for all parties. Parents try to talk children into attending classes or even force them to. Many in Ukraine consider gymnastics a prestigious sport; they think it makes a person disciplined and assertive. It does. But if your child dreams of drawing or singing, sculpting in clay, or embroidering, it's better to avoid pushing them into the world of enormous and painful stretching.

The second most widespread mistake is setting unrealistic goals. For example, some parents demand that their children win competitions and get medals very young. I know many cases when parents of six years old children would endlessly ask coaches about when their daughter would become a world champion. I advise not to do this because otherwise, the children live under the weight of someone else's expectations in the sport they may not even like.

Now that I am a mother, I understand how crucial to discover your child's interest in something. Take notice of a child's potential, what they like, what they enjoy doing, and what they can do the best.

I chose Rhythmic Gymnastics for myself. Yes, I started because my Mom was a coach, but initially, I just wanted to dance all the time. And my parents arranged everything smartly: they found what I liked and brought me to the gym. But, of course, they had their doubts initially and considered ballet or any other dance for me.

My parents always supported me throughout my career; they never pressured me to go for medals. Even if Mom sometimes gave me critical feedback, Dad was always on my side. I was always the best for him, whether in the gym or at home. It is essential when your closest ones believe in you and can find the right words no matter what. It is a gift when your family loves your hobby as much as you do. I was lucky to have that.

Dad would explain to me from a very young age that working hard and doing your job well is necessary. He believed that coming to the gym first, leaving last, and exercising at home would eventually lead to success.
"Work more than others, do not feel sorry for yourself." Dad would constantly put these ideas into my head.

Motivation is essential, and you can't force it. Finding the right way to make your child interested in something is better. You may start with games. For example, a child has to show their wish to attend a club. Then think if that kind of activity suits your child's physical and mental state. And if a child is eager to try, help them.

When I was five, I loved Rhythmic Gymnastics so much that I begged my parents to bring me to the gym. And only after a few years I experienced a crisis point when my parents forced me to work harder. But later, when I became much older, I realized their strictness was necessary for my career.

Keep in mind that our sport is young. Girls usually finish their careers by 21. So, if you want to succeed in it, you have to be a dedicated child. It's not easy even for adults to make tremendous physical efforts continuously, much less for a child.

37

The parent's role is to explain all whys. When people are born, they don't understand that they need to work. All those notions were put into my head by Mom and Dad, and for that, I am grateful. I was lucky to be born into an athletic family. Mom did Rhythmic Gymnastics, and Dad was a swimmer. Thanks to their background, I got involved in the sport when I was knee-high.

Getting dedicated to professional sports at fourteen-fifteen, but not at seven or eight. And when you are serious, it's better to shift to distance learning. Combining school and a young athlete's career is extremely hard, especially in such a young sport as Gymnastics. So I suggest profoundly thinking about what might be a life-changing decision.

But do not take primary school years away from a child. I often watch parents sending children to distance learning in the first grade, counting on the sport. It is not correct and even harmful. No one knows what the future holds, and any sport is unpredictable. Therefore, it is vital to combine sports and school in early grades.

In Simferopol, I had first problems with my studies in the sixth year of secondary school, but somehow, I coped with that. However, being in Kyiv, at the Deriugina School, required complete devotion. We lived and studied in the school's dormitory.

Teachers didn't cut us any slack. We had to use breaks and free hours after the training to do school homework. There, the sport was in first place and education in second. But those are the sacrifices professional athletes are willing to make.

Lastly, I encourage parents to make decisions relying on inner feelings and intuition, not rigid logic. For example, when you bring your child to any sports club, and a coach tells you that your child hasn't got the appropriate criteria, lacks natural talent, and, in general, is not the right fit, do not give up. Again, I am objective evidence: coaches can be wrong. It's the dedication that makes an athlete, not just raw talent.

Based on what nature gave me, I wasn't born for Rhythmic Gymnastics: inappropriate leg length, too skinny, etc. Rhythmic gymnasts are not just girls with long legs. They look like models. But my figure happened to be a different shape.

However, my parents believed in me, so I achieved my goals through hard work and persistence. It is because I wanted to be a gymnast more than anything.

If your child is keen, never give up. Even if the legs are not the right length, work hard, do pirouettes, and practice so the body can grow and reshape. There are a significant number of specialists who may help, including doctors and physical therapists. The twenty-first century is a time of opportunities for all.

CHAPTER 10

APPROACHING THE DERIUGINA SCHOOL

Ukraine is famous for its gymnasts. The school, founded by Albina Deriugina and Iryna Deriugina, is recognized worldwide. Many girls dream of going to the famous Deriugina school.

I wasn't the exception. All girls from the gym where I trained were fascinated by any performance of Deriugina's gymnasts. And it was for a reason. The girls who went there were slender, with long legs, splendid stretching skills, and exceptionally artistically expressive. They were the best of the best. Gymnasts from remote cities looked at them with wide-open eyes; they were levels above us all. They were gods, and we were mortal; this is how we felt. And, of course, everybody strived to get to Kyiv.

At the Ukrainian Championship, I got third place after gymnasts from the Deriugina school. At that competition, I was the youngest. The other girls were at least two years older than me. That victory helped me to find courage and confidence. My so-called trauma about being a coach's daughter, caused by constant critique, was finally fading away.

Yes, I was a coach's daughter, but I did my best and exceeded others. Besides, some had my Mom as a coach too. Since then, I realized that I could do something and could do it well if I became third in the nationals.

My whole family was happy. Even the fact that I got approved for such a big competition already became a landmark event. Joining the Big League of Ukrainian Rhythmic Gymnastics was almost impossible back then. However, Albina Deriugina was at every big contest and personally watched every gymnast.

After the championship, she noticed me and started to follow my results. I won the subsequent competition among the gymnasts born the same year as me, 1993. It was in Kharkiv. I won with the highest total score by performing six routines (free hands, rope, hoop, ball, clubs, and ribbon).

According to international rules, juniors were to compete in four events, but Albina Deriugina set her own rules for the Ukrainian championships. Whether young or adult gymnasts, you had to perform in all six. Naturally, not everybody fancied the idea; many complained. "Can we at least skip the rope?" they would ask. But Albina Deriugina was confident that every gymnast had to perform well in all disciplines.

I won the first prize in the contest, exceeding the girls from Kyiv. It meant a lot to me. People rumored again about my Mom and me. Simferopol is a city with a country lifestyle, and I couldn't escape those rumors anymore. I wanted to get rid of that as soon as possible. Only in the Deriugina School in Kyiv was it possible if they would take me.

After the Championship of Ukraine, Albina Deriugina invited me to Kyiv. The dream came true! Mom had already prepared many students for the Deriugina School, such as Elena Gatilova, Veronika Belyaeva, and Olena Dzubchuk, all medallists of the World Championships. Also, Viktoria Antonova, Anna Subbotina, Oleksandra Gridasova.

Mom heard a lot about difficulties one might face in that 'rigorous' school and worried a lot for me; she had concerns about whether I could withstand the pressure. We postponed moving to Kyiv, but both understood it was inevitable.

One more critical competition for me was the Deriugina Cup. I was still training under my Mom's command but was already a Junior Ukrainian National Team member. The contest was traditionally held in the capital city, in March, on Albina Deriugina's birthday.

Supposing the Deriugina school was a far-fetched dream, the Deriugina Cup was unfeasible.

Mom went to every Deriugina Cup; she brought magazines, notebooks, and signed posters by Ukrainian celebrities. I never even thought of competing there. But the Derigunas imposed an innovation: they invited ten gifted junior gymnasts from around Ukraine to the competition. So we had to show our two best routines and participated in the contest.

Figure 9. Team Bronze in European Championship, 2008. Tetyana Zavhorodnya, Viktoria Mazur, Anna Rizatdinova

Ania Subbotina and I represented Crimea. Before that, we trained like astronauts: strenuous, challenging training from morning till night. Having observed Kyiv's methods, Mom followed them. People called the training technique 'an unbearable torture.'

The training program made by Albina Deriugina was called 'seven-five-four-two' and consisted of endless repetition of the performance routines.

Even though the gymnasts hated it, it worked. Upon the 'seven-five-four-two,' we were ready for any competition and to fly to Mars if necessary.

The system was the following: first, performing with a hoop, repeating seven times. Afterward, a gymnast took a ball and repeated it five times. Same with clubs, but four times. And, finally, ribbon, two times. All these we had to do without breaks. It was long and strenuous work to train endurance.

On the next training day, the system changed. The last exercise became the first. After that, we started with a ribbon seven times, and so on.

Even after a few weeks of working in such mode, the one obtains increased focus of movements and accuracy and becomes aware of every step. In Kyiv, they used this program to train adult gymnasts; then, in Crimea, Mom set up her know-how to make junior gymnasts follow the system.

I was preparing for the Deriugina Cup in a particular way. There were clubs and a hoop in my program. On the first day of the competition, I flawlessly performed two of my routines, and frankly speaking, I was curious to know if someone liked me. They also asked a few more girls and me to perform the following day. Then, we had to choose the best routine for one more exhibition performance. My Mom and I were over the Moon because I got noticed among the other ten junior gymnasts and put into the schedule on the day of finals.

It was so honorable! I was so excited I couldn't sleep. I decided to go with clubs; it was my strongest. I started performing and lost a club while doing the simplest element, "the mill." I absorbed dance and lost balance; a club landed beyond the stage. I had to run to pick it up. That was my debut at the international level competitions.

I thought it was the end of my career. Everybody tried comforting me and told me I was performing just an exhibition. But I felt so embarrassed that I never wanted to perform again, especially in front of the Deriuginas. I thought I would be excluded from the

Junior National Team, to which I got accepted after the championship in Dnipro. It felt like my career was over, and it was time to say goodbye to Rhythmic Gymnastics.

Fortunately, in a few days, I calmed down and started preparing for the next competition. Then there was a selection of athletes born in 1992-1993 to the European Championship 2007 in group events with five clubs. I fit right in. The three best gymnasts from Kyiv were from the Deriugina's school, and two were from Crimea. It was honorable and scary simultaneously. I was only partially aware of the European Championships.

Albina Deriugina and Iryna Deriugina decided that the junior team had to train in Simferopol with my Mom and a few more coaches. Not to interfere with the training process of other gymnasts, we went to Crimea. It was strenuous group work. We became one team with the girls from Kyiv. Only then we realized they were humans, too.

After, we went back to the capital city. I once met Albina Deriugina at the Ukrainian championships. But there, in Kyiv, I saw her daughter, Iryna Deriugina, for the first time. We showed her our routines, and she made some changes. She seemed to me very beautiful and stylish and had her ultimate fashion. But a little later, she commented on everything and criticized our performances, although they were flawless from our point of view.

We were preparing in Kyiv for the final week and a half before the European Championship. I dreamed of training with Natalia Godunko and Anna Bessonova, who I have admired since childhood. There were tons of posters with their photos in my room in Simferopol; that was how much I loved them, especially Bessonova. To see with my own eyes how they trained was extremely important for me. I didn't go out for a break; I watched them from the corner. I was interested in their every move: how they entered the gym, warmed up, what bags they were carrying, and what clothes they wore.

And if Ania or Natasha commented on somebody's performance, it meant a lot. I worried wildly. I would feel stressed, especially when Godunko would say something; if she started commenting. However, my deep respect for these gymnasts was evident.

At the end of June, our group attended the European Rhythmic Gymnastics Championship in Baku, Azerbaijan. We were given team wear and went there as a part of the National Team. It was big responsibility and honor.

Athletes from thirty-three countries performed there, at the Heydar Aliyev Sports and Exhibition Complex. We won fifth place in a group exercise with five clubs. But ambitions were too high at that age. We felt like it was a failure. We thought we deserved more. Now I realize that fifth place was a good result at the time. I am grateful to God that I had the opportunity to train and perform with those gymnasts. It was a fresh impetus for my further growth.

After the competition, my family and I went to Turkey on vacation. Later I started to prepare for the twenty-fourth Rhythmic Gymnastics European Championships in Turin, but only in individual all-around events. However, I still trained with Mom. It was the end of 2008.

Group events were always more complicated for me than the individual; I was tense because I had to adjust to every other gymnast. There wasn't only one leader on the mat, there were five, and we all were a team. So I was always afraid to let somebody down. But I always sought the limelight; I wanted the audience to watch only myself. So I have always dreamt of performing individually.

There were many to choose from based on the results of the Ukrainian Championships. Albina Deriugina decided that Anna Rizatdinova from Crimea, Tetiana Zahorodnia from Lviv, and Viktoria Mazur from Kyiv would attend the European Championship in Turin.

My Mom was very nervous; she was present during the whole preparation process, examining my every step. She constantly checked my weight because other girls were skinny, especially

Viktoria Mazur. On the other hand, I was taller, a year older, and more experienced than Viktoria.

At first, we trained for Turin in Crimea; later, I came to Kyiv. In Turin, I felt uncontrollable fear. But, frankly, the group event wasn't as scary as an individual one. So, naturally, my ambitions were high, and I dreamt of a gold medal.

The championship program was the following: the Ukrainian team had to perform four disciplines in medal group events. Then, the trainers' Council decided that I, being the reigning champion of Ukraine, had to perform two routines, with hoop and ribbon. After that, Tetiana Zahorodnia performed a rope routine, and Viktoria Mazur did the ball. This squad was going after medals.

Then, the judges counted points from all four exercises, and the sum determined our place at the championship. As a team, we got bronze medals. It was the first significant medal in my collection! It was somewhat unexpected, and I felt on top of the world: the second big championship for me, and we won! For other girls, that championship was the first.

Final individual performances were scheduled for the following day when I performed with hoop and ribbon; I consequently won fourth and fifth place. However, I felt miserable, just a few steps from the top three. I wanted to be among the prize takers, but I failed. I remember being heartbroken, but I admit, it was a great experience.

CHAPTER 11

INDIVIDUAL EVENTS? NOT GOING TO HAPPEN

I enrolled at the school of Deriuginas and moved to Kyiv in January 2009. Mom realized I had to be a good fit for the school, which, naturally, meant extreme weight management. I was in perfect shape. My height was 5'7" (170 cm), and my weight was 99 lb (45 kg). The only disproportion was that I was taller than other girls.

I still remember the first day at school. After entering the gym, I walked up to Albina Deriugina. She genuinely brightened up.

"Indeed, we are delighted to have you here, Annushka," she said. After hearing those warm and homey words, I felt calm and relaxed. It almost felt like she welcomed not just any child but her daughter back home. It seemed like I would get used to Kyiv, and eventually, the Deriugina School would become my second home.

Then, I walked up to Iryna Deriugina, who seemed very strict. I was scared. Fear even made me sweat. Finally, she told me, "Young lady, you look considerably bigger since the Junior European Championship." She immediately tamed my childish excitement by highlighting my long body and wide for the gymnast's hips and shoulders. That was how we first met.

Later, Iryna Deriugina had a private chat with my Mom. The verdict was harsh and not negotiable. "Annie may be suitable to perform in group events, and it is only because we deeply respect you and your work, Oksana," she told my Mom.

It meant I would miss the first string. Mom was sad but politely replied, "Thank you, we appreciate it." Then, naturally, she didn't say anything to me. But, when I suddenly had to learn a group routine in the third string, it all became clear to me.

I was devastated; I didn't want to perform in a group, not even in the first string. I had been dreaming of performing individually for years. But the reality was different, and I had to cope.

Then I realized that Iryna Deriugina didn't see any talent in me; therefore, I had no hope of ever performing individual events. Around thirty gymnasts were training in the school. Still, only Anna Bessonova, Alina Maksymenko, Daria Kushnerova, Valeria Shurkhal, and Viktoria Lenyshyn were fit for individual events; they were the pleiad of talented gymnasts. So there was no space for me in that temple of fame.

After a month, in February 2009, I went to Estonia to participate in an international contest. I was surprised I got to go; probably one of the gymnasts got sick and needed a replacement. We went with Alina Maksymenko to the Baltics. I had to perform my old Crimean program.

There, we saw the most prominent gymnasts worldwide, for instance, Evgeniya Kanaeva, who became an Olympic champion in Beijing. I performed four routines with rope, hoop, ball, and ribbon. In general, I did well. I exceeded Alina Maksymenko, who was two years older than me. I brought home silver and gold medals given for the finals. It was my triumph!

Considering that the Olympic champion took first place, and I was still a relatively unknown gymnast, taking two medals was unbelievable!

However, I was very disappointed when nobody recognized my achievements in Kyiv. I hoped to get into individual events and start more intensive training. But the school had different plans for me. Iryna Deriugina insisted, "Your top is group events. Keep silent and work; perhaps we will try you for something else one day."

After some time, I was accepted to the first string and joined the team with which we went to Thiais, France, to participate in the Grand Prix series competition. In 2008 I had been performing a group routine as part of a junior team, but this time I was a member of the adult National Team.

My program included two routines: one with three ribbons and two ropes, and the second had five hoops. But, honestly, we performed poorly. We had a mixed team: older and younger girls, and we could not work as a real team. Moreover, we needed more time to prepare. And as a result, we failed.

After returning to Kyiv, we had the Deriugina Cup 2009 ahead of us. Before the start, the school decided that Valeria Shurkhal and I were to perform group and individual routines.

"What if you both present your individuals out of the competition?" Albina Deriugina suggested. I was thrilled to hear that, realizing it was an excellent chance to demonstrate my skills.

At the Deriugina Cup, Anna Bessonova competed as the first number of the National Team, Alina Maksymenko was second, Valeria Shurkhal, Daria Kushnerova, and I were third, fourth, and fifth numbers consequently.

The first day of the competition began. I was performing rope, hoop, ball, and ribbon routines. It turned out that Alina Maksymenko made a severe mistake in her ball routine at the qualifications stage. Nobody is immune from making mistakes, especially in sports. Nevertheless, I performed with flying colors; my score was higher than Alina's. For this reason, two gymnasts made it to the final: Anna Bessonova under the first number and me under the second. And this was how I got to the FIG World Rankings.

If an all-around gymnast gets to the final, she becomes among the best eight gymnasts of each apparatus. After that, she starts competing in the Grand Prix series. It means that the organizer covers financial expenses, except for tickets. Usually, there are up to ten Grand Prix competitions organized each year.

You will get many opportunities if you appear among the best eight gymnasts at least in one routine. Then, you are in the top eight.

I secured my place by attending the Deriugina Cup final. I finally had a future! After that, Ukraine could be represented by three gymnasts in the Grand Prix series: Anna Bessonova, Alina Maksymenko, and Anna Rizatdinova. What a pleasure it was for my family and me! Finally, our years-long efforts started to pay off.

Traditionally, a grand gala concert is hosted on the final day of the Deriugina Cup. However, that day, Iryna Deriugina announced a competition: only the best of the best would become a part of a big upcoming performance called Carmina Burana. She needed four girls.

I worked day and night to become one of the four. But eventually, Iryna Deriugina chose her favorites, and I wasn't one of them. I remember how sad I was. But, at the same time, I knew I would not give up.

CHAPTER 12

LIVING ON MY OWN

In Kyiv, I started to live on my own. I had to tackle difficulties by myself. I was the only child in my family, so I was raised with love; everyone adored me and treated me with care. It was hard for my parents to let me go. At first, they were thinking about renting me an apartment. Still, Albina Deriugina said, "If you want Annie to become a responsible person and a good athlete, you have to settle her in the same conditions as everybody else; she has to share the housing with her team and not stand out."

Naturally, my parents considered Albina Deriugina's advice. As a result, the Republican Higher Vocational School of Physical Training and Sports boarding school became my new home. Of course, living conditions were far from perfect, but they were equal for every girl on the National Team.

The boarding school was located next to the Lisova underground station. Therefore, our gym trip took around 30-40 minutes every day.

It was like an army. We had a housemistress who maintained the order. The lights were off at 10 p.m. every day. The room had nothing except a wardrobe, table, chairs, bedside tables, and beds. There were no electronic devices except plugs for charging phones.

We had one shared bathroom and often had to wait in line. We ate at the canteen. Live conditions were spartan, but they made me independent and strong-willed, and I discovered a great sense of humor.

In the beginning, I missed my parents a lot. They visited me once every two months. They both worked and couldn't come to the capital more often. So, they would stay in the Corona Hotel next to the boarding school when they came to Kyiv. And then, we would spend some time together. It was delightful!

A bit later, coaches and management decided to create more comfortable living conditions for gymnasts. The most promising athletes moved to the Corona Hotel. Thus, I lived with Viktoria Mazur in one room. We were overjoyed as we finally got home appliances: a fridge, a TV, and a bathroom right in the room. But it only happened in 2011.

Back in 2009, I lived in an old-fashioned boarding school, in an austere room, and would go to the city center by subway every day. I would get off at Khreshchatyk station and then run to Instytutska Street. After showing promising results at the Deriugina Cup, I was passionate about the future.

There was a thorough preparation for the European Championship in Baku, where gymnasts had to meet to compete for a team medal set and for the finals. Almost every week, we went through checkpoints. The coaches couldn't decide who should go to the Championship.

At first, they agreed on Anna Bessonova, Alina Maksymenko, and Valeria Shurkhal, but then they considered me. Finally, they decided that Anna Bessonova would present four routines, and Maksymenko would perform three or four. The exact number of performances was still uncertain. If Alina performed three, Valeria Shurkhal or I would perform with a ribbon. We were good at pirouettes, which was necessary for a ribbon routine.

But simultaneously, I realized I had no chance to attend the competition because Valeria was one of Iryna Deriugina's favorites. I could see how much time she devoted to coaching her individually. In contrast, I still had my outdated Crimean program.

The Deriuginas often invited coaches from all around the country to prepare gymnasts for competitions. I was lucky enough to train with Olha Melnytska from Luhansk in May. She then offered a strict training process, and we worked hard doing 10-10.

One day Iryna Deriugina finally decided to work with me. She said, "Now we are going to modify your routine." She intended to make Valeria work better this way, to make her stay focused and realize she had a rival behind her. I tried my best. As it was the first time, Iryna Deriugina asked me to perform on the main floor to see my program. My heart rate exceeded 220 beats per minute.

"This is my chance," I thought. But unfortunately, I made a false step right after the start. I fell. The coach chuckled softly, adding, "The kid is trying so hard that she even goes weak in her knees."

The leader of our National Team, Anna Bessonova, was helping me out that day. First, she showed me some new movements. Then, we chose the Ukrainian national song Hopak for the ribbon routine. I was over the moon, trying so hard that it seemed like I was ready to take off. The thought that I was finally performing on the leading carpet under Iryna Deriugina's supervision inspired me greatly.

At last, we modified my old program. I successfully presented myself at all three checking points. I was chosen to attend the European Championship instead of Valeria Shurkhal. I was stunned by the news and couldn't believe I was so lucky.

We arrived in Baku. The day before the contest at the evening training Albina Deriugina told me, "We decided that you are not going to perform tomorrow. We need good results for our team, but you are still a very young gymnast; we can't risk it. So stay in the stands and help to support the girls". I agreed and didn't take any offense.

Anna Bessonova and Alina Maksymenko were older than me and, undoubtedly, much more experienced. The coach was right. After the girls performed four routines, the team got third place. I was devotedly rooting for them. That's what my first European Rhythmic Gymnastics championship looked like.

But since I was the third number on our team, I also got a medal according to the rules. Upon completing the contest, Anna

Bessonova and Alina Maksymenko got their medals at the awards ceremony; I got mine at the party later. I was pleased but realized that I didn't earn that award. I was in a strong team but wasn't that strong yet.

CHAPTER 13

NO PAIN, NO GAIN

Upon returning to Kyiv, I decided to gain Iryna Deriugina's trust and respect. It was a long and arduous journey. All my efforts were in vain at first. I wasn't fit for her standards. I knew I couldn't win her favor with a perfect figure, beautiful legs, body curves, or theatrical facial expressions that she usually appreciated. So, I got only one option: to gain her affection by working hard and showing a tremendous desire to do Rhythmic Gymnastics. It took years, but eventually, I managed to succeed.

Most other students and I were sent to the second carpet during the early years of training at the school. For example, Iryna Deriugina would come to the gym and say, "Do 10-10, along with blushing cheeks. Right after your face becomes red, come to see me".

No doubt, I used to be among the first. It was my chance. I would complete every 10-10 of each routine and run to the coach red-faced. It worked like this: we divided our routine into two parts, did the first part 10 times, then the second 10 more times. At first, she never showed any reaction, but as time passed, my persistence began to raise her interest; she could notice how hard the kid on the second carpet was trying. Sometimes I would even be an example of diligence for the rest of the group. But still, Iryna Deriugina was captivated by beautiful, vivid gymnasts, and I wasn't on the list. Regardless of what I did, other girls were a priority.

I didn't train on the leading carpet, designed for more talented students, for a long time. Feeling like a misfit, I kept exercising, having no hope of succeeding one day. I was staying on the second carpet doing dull 'donkey work.' It became normal.

Once, a glimmer of hope appeared. I got invited to train on the central carpet from time to time. Of course, I was delighted because my efforts finally paid off. But time passed, and it looked like Iryna Deriugina was doing that to motivate other girls to work harder. She probably thought that hardworking Rizatdinova would start up an engine creating a buzzing atmosphere. Nevertheless, I kept my spirits up, realizing it was an excellent chance to put my best foot forward.

Suddenly a miracle happened! One day, Iryna Deriugina asked me to present my performance to music during the dry run. I was trying so hard that it seemed I might jump out of my leotard. Fear and an overwhelming desire to prove myself were raging inside of me. While performing, I could feel every muscle in my body. I was on fire. Even my fingers were tense. After that dry run, Iryna Deriugina complimented me on doing my best. The following day I could not get out of bed. I was physically and emotionally exhausted.

Even though I was still more like an instrument to motivate others, Iryna Deriugina invited me to train on the central carpet more often. Of course, it meant a lot to me. However, I was jealous when I saw the coach spending much more time with other girls, even after school. It sometimes even seemed that girls didn't appreciate her efforts enough. On the contrary, I would do anything to train with Iryna Deriugina.

The 2009 World Rhythmic Gymnastics Championships in Mie, Japan, was coming. We had to compete for a team award with a total score of twenty routines. Anna Bessonova and Alina Maksymenko represented Ukraine. Daria Kushnerova and I were prepared to become the third number on the team.

We worked from morning till night following Albina Deriugina's plan 7-5-4-2. I even found setting myself up for that number of dry runs difficult. But I realized that there was no way back. Every preparation for the European or World Championship began with this method. I was not too fond of that plan but later realized it worked like a charm. It was created right for me. After 7-5-4-2, I was fit and ready to go to any championship.

During the time, there was a conflict between the head coach and my fellow gymnast. Following the educational objective and to set an example for others, Albina Deriugina suspended Daria Kushnerova from the World Championship. Upon that, the coaches decided to send me as the third number of the team to Mie.

Bessonova, Maksymenko, and Rizatdinova were to present four routines. I realized what a burden I had to carry; I had to perform as a part of the team, and I couldn't let the other's down. As a team, we could become contenders for awards.

The final part of the preparation period was exhausting. We wouldn't even smile; we cried and didn't talk to each other. We were just like robots, endlessly repeating the 7-5-4-2 exercise. We were running out of time. Then, in the final evening training session, right before the flight, I sprained my ankle during the second of seven repetitions of the ball routine. While balancing on my toes, I heard a crackling sound in my left foot; it sounded like a broken branch. I got scared and fell. Doctors and massage therapists immediately ran up to me. The music stopped.

The girls tried to help; Bessonova brought an ice pack and Alina some gauze rolls. Unfortunately, it was a ligament tear, and I suffered a lot later. Any exercise caused severe pain in the foot. Only after the accident Albina Deriugina canceled her 7-5-4-2 plan. She understood that it was too much. The following day we flew to Japan.

I was extremely nervous because of the upcoming performance together in one team with such a celebrity as Anna Bessonova. My main concern was to do everything without mistakes. I performed well but did not get good scores and didn't get in the top 10. Even with Bessonova, we still needed to work hard for team awards.

It was an unpleasant surprise and a great disappointment. But Bessonova performed with flying colors in the final. She got only a bronze medal, but everyone chanted, "Ukraine!". Alina Maksymenko and I were so nervous we even cried.

Sure thing, I was disappointed by my performance. I understood that I did everything well, yet my score was poor. For the first time, I started to second-guess if the professional sport was right for me. I was so far from the top places. So what was the reason for going through all those exhausting training sessions? Luckily, the thought quickly flew away.

Figure 10. My first senior individual program. Japan, 2009. Gymnasts: Anna Rizatdinova, Anna Bessonova, Alina Maksimenko

After the Championship, Iryna Deriugina told my Mom, "Annie performed well; she didn't let the team down."

"But I still think she would do better in group events. The individuals are too tough for her. She lacks some catchy traits", she added. Mom didn't share it with me, but she got distraught; she cried a lot. She felt bad because she knew I liked the sport and how hard I worked for individual events.

CHAPTER 14

EXPRESS YOURSELF

"You do everything like an excellent student; it's rather boring. Use emotional paints to color and express yourself", Iryna Deriugina constantly reminded me. The meaning of these words seemed so vague that I couldn't come up with a solution. I did my best every day at the training; I was red-faced after every session and did all the given tasks. It seemed to me that I was expressing myself in performances just fine.

Peers and coaches told me that I got a problem with adult emotions. They called me a mouse. I took criticism very close to my heart; it seemed unfair. Mouse? How could I be compared to a mouse if emotions raged inside me? Only later I realized that professional gymnastics required mature emotions, almost like professional acting.

I was lucky enough to watch the performances of our National Team celebrities. At the World Championship in Japan, I performed side by side with the legendary Anna Bessonova. Unfortunately, she left the professional sport after that competition. However, her level of proficiency was what I wanted to achieve. After she left, Alina Maksymenko became number one on the National Team. She was naturally very expressive. So, there was no need to teach her that.

Iryna Deriugina was looking for emotional expressivity in every gymnast. She often said, "You have to live the story on the stage; you get one minute and thirty seconds for that."

It was challenging for me. Therefore, Iryna Deriugina made me come to the big mirror on the second carpet and perform a routine, watching myself. "Do it until you believe your reflection," she asked.

During the performance, a gymnast can't look down. But it often happens when athletes try too hard to do all the elements technically well, managing the apparatus or counting points in their heads.

"Just imagine that there are spectators and judges around you, and you aim to charm them," said Iryna Deriugina. "They want to enjoy your performance. Get your eyes off the floor! Show them your eyes, your smile, your passion!"

Iryna Deriugina was right; standing out is crucial in our sport. When people ask how to become a Rhythmic Gymnastics star, I always say that one needs more than good flexibility, expressivity, and a strong desire. You have to have it all. This kind of sport is too diverse. It may seem easy at first glance, but combining all components is challenging.

At the age of 18-19, I was a hardworking girl with an average gymnast body and immense motivation, but judges never liked me. They didn't notice me and always graded me low. In Rhythmic Gymnastics, it is vital to be striking, eye-catching, with vivid emotions. Standing out is a part of success.

Iryna Deriugina thought I had no distinguishing characteristics and lacked something unique. But then, I looked like twenty more other gymnasts, my rivals at the Championship. I needed catchy traits to climb the ranking ladder. Several years had passed before Iryna Deriugina noticed me and helped me find my style, feel the music more profoundly, and grow emotionality.

It wasn't easy. The coach tried me in different styles: classics, rock, and Ukrainian folklore. We looked desperately and tried everything. But it was an actual act of creation, and I adored it.

CHAPTER 15

THE GIRLS' ARMY

Initially, the Deriugina School was established in Kyiv in 1996. Nowadays, it is well-known all over the world. This school has always been a trendsetter in the world of Rhythmic Gymnastics. Iryna Deriugina and Albina Deriugina are the founders and permanent coaches.

The school is a top-notch brand of teachers' talent and professionalism, students' aptitude, and never-ending creative pursuits. However, behind every student's astonishing performance, strict rules are obligatory for everyone. The Olympic Champions train there, and so does the National Team. The greatest coaches of Ukraine send their athletes here from other cities.

Indeed, the Deriugina School is a proper place for strong-willed athletes with good endurance abilities. No wonder we have earned the nickname "the girls' army." We are often compared to Dynamo football school, named after Valeriy Lobanovskyi. Only the strongest may survive based on their physical and mental abilities.

Our daily routine was challenging. The training began at 8:30 a.m. and ended at 7 p.m. We hurried to check our weight as soon as we entered the school.

Albina Deriugina used to come first and was always ready for instant action. Before the start, we would hear, "Dress! Attention! About turn!". It was a mini-army for girls, our boot camp. After, we would start working out. First, we got down to a skipping rope exercise along with running. Then, we proceeded with the Amerykanka warm-up routine, a choreography floor lesson. It included activities to increase flexibility and mobility skills to work out all muscle groups – from the foot to the neck. It took one hour and a half.

The Amerykanka was combined with power exercises. Usually, a Rhythmic Gymnastics warm-up begins with a choreography lesson worldwide. The most prominent choreographers from Dnipro and Odesa used to come to our school, too. But Albina Deriugina didn't recognize any other warm-up because she saw its effect. So, for this reason, we did it all the time.

The coach considered these exercises great for warming up and injury prevention. However, without a break, we had to repeat all the movements 16 times, sometimes even 24 times. Moreover, the legs had 1lb (500g) weight cuffs—quite challenging.

Typically, we would burn up to 1 or 2lb (500g or 1kg) of fat during one warm-up like this. By the end, I was out of breath. Albina Mykolaivna was always loudly counting our movements, correcting everyone. In classes, I always tried staying on the front line. I used to lie before the coach and follow her counting, and I enjoyed it.

Albina Deriugina's warm-ups are known all around the world. She constantly repeated, "Even if the body is imperfect, you can fix it by doing floor exercises." So I concluded that I had to do my best in performing Amerykanka. Thus, I could improve the health of my legs and make them longer, make the hips tighter, and fix flaws.

After the Amerykanka, the coach usually divided us into two groups, 15 girls each. Standing in line, we would do another of Albina Deriugina's favorite exercises, jumps and leaps. Ukrainian gymnasts have always been famous for their great leaps. In addition, they have demonstrated an extraordinary ability to maintain the body's advanced position while performing the jump, to make it look like flying.

Many ask what my secret is. I always respond daily and yearly; I have done jumps and leaps in every training session. Usually, Viktoria Mazur was in the front. It was always challenging for me to do the jumps. So, Albina Deriugina put me next to Viktoria to look up to her. We used to do it for two hours without breaks. It was almost unbearable. Sometimes I couldn't breathe. Even when feeling side stitches, we weren't allowed to stop. If we performed poorly, Albina Deriugina would be in a bad mood the whole day.

In many countries, warm-up exercises are somewhat important, only an hour long. After athletes warm their muscles, do whatever prep they need and start working with the apparatus. Our National Team dedicates more than an hour to the Amerykanka, then an hour or an hour and a half for leaps. It equals three to four hours of total warm-up.

Iryna Deriugina was there around noon to work on individual programs. First, we had to practice with apparatus to music. Then, we were so exhausted after doing the leaps we could barely walk to the second weight check. After such busy mornings, we were willing to rest for a while, but the coach was waiting, so the work continued.

Usually, we practiced four routines. During the day, we had a hoop, a ball, and a ribbon; clubs were left for the evening. If we were training for a big contest, we would do four routines during the day and four in the evening. Then, we would complete the program under Albina or Iryna Deriugina's supervision and go to another weight check.

After, we would go to the changing room. We had some rest: napped, did home assignments, watched movies, read books, and snacked. However, it was only a half break because, at any time, we could be back to practice. We had to get up if the coach walked in. And only after we would hear, "You may take your seats and have a meal," it was a real break.

Albina Deriugina didn't like it when somebody was sleeping or lying down during the break. So everyone tried to sit rather than lie down when she was around. Sometimes we had to show what was in our bags. It happened relatively rarely, only before some severe competitions. The coaches did it because they feared some 'illegal' items, like sweets.

We used to bring some snacks for lunch, and some girls had a bar of chocolate, waffle, or cookies. All sweets and sodas, which were also 'illegal,' were confiscated. The coaches would take the 'illegal' bag to identify and punish the rule breakers.

After the training, we had a final weight check. Gymnasts spent in the gym all day long, almost without leaving the October Palace. We would leave at 7 p.m. The younger ones could have dinner a little earlier. We only used to get to the dormitory around 8 p.m. by taking the underground. However, sometimes we would miss the last train. So, we stayed in the changing rooms and slept on the sofas.

We followed this schedule six days a week. Sunday was our only day off. However, I often went to the gym on Sundays to practice. It didn't bother me; I understood the importance.

The school rules were strict. Albina and Iryna Deriuginas were our commanding officers. Everyone feared them, so no one tried to object or disobey them. No one even could think about it. Talking during the training or turning away from the coach was forbidden. No laughs and no jokes.

If you meet one of the Deriuginas anywhere, you have to say "hi"; if you leave, say "goodbye" and always say "thank you." We knew that a teacher was an absolute authority who was always right. So we took their advice and were thankful.

Mondays were tough because, after the weekend, the weight would go up. I was very young when I moved to Kyiv, and I remember how hard it was to make myself work at full stretch. A holiday is a disaster for a gymnast. Even after having only one day off, it takes a few more days to get back to a regular schedule. Albina Deriugina hated any time-wasting activities like parties or clubbing. She could read bodies and instantly saw what you had done the day before, sleeping, partying, or dancing in the club till the morning. It was impossible to trick her.

There was one more unspoken rule: once in school, you should not have romantic relationships. The coaches clarified that any relationships would negatively affect the training process. So we were not even allowed to think about the outer world in the gym. Instead, we had to concentrate on the sport. They said it because gymnastics is a sport for the young, and if you want to achieve something big, it requires an absolute commitment.

Anyway, some girls were seeing boys, but they kept it secret. On the contrary, I couldn't even think about dating someone. After each training session, I was so tired I just wanted to go home.

Occasionally, there are some articles in the media about so-called bullying and the humiliating treatment of juniors in our school. But I don't see it this way. Older gymnasts would give some tasks to younger ones. For instance, ask them to run to groceries for forbidden sweets. We always had an amicable and healthy relationship. After all, we were one family. We had a powerful bond inside our Rhythmic Gymnastics team. We often defended or even told little lies to cover for each other. I was never afraid of the older girls; I respected them.

Every gymnast had to have a personal sports diary. This rule was obligatory. Sometimes, older girls could ask to do it for them. Albina Deriugina gave us detailed instructions on journaling. We had to write about the daily routine, physical well-being, blood pressure, weight, general physical and mental state, and mistakes analysis. We were supposed to write down everything she said to analyze her words. When we knew someone was watching us, we would journal, but never otherwise.

Once, we stopped journaling for a month. Then, Albina Deriugina asked us to bring our journals to the next class. Panic broke out: some forgot to take it, and some hurriedly wrote something down. An empty journal would make Albina Mykolaivna very angry.

The looks and appearance were important. A gymnast had to look neat with hair styled in a bun, wearing a clean black uniform. Colorful clothes were not desirable. White socks, shoes without holes, and a leotard with a waistband were part of our working clothes.

After we finished the training, it was necessary to collect all apparatus. Athletes on duty cleaned up the mess. If something was not in order, we got punished.

Once a year, the school held a meeting of the Executive Committee. Albina Deriugina personally chose members: coaches from different cities in Ukraine. All guilty girls were to come to the accountant's office, where the meeting occurred. It looked like a trial. The guilty person was in the middle of the room, the 'jury' coaches were standing around her, and they were investigating the 'victim' by asking, "Why don't you work at full stretch? What hinders you?"

Sometimes, the main aim of the Executive Committee was to get a gymnast down by testing her patience. The coaches wanted to discuss everyone's weight problems, careless attitude to exercises, and wrong behavior. The guilty person usually returned sobbing and crying.

But it all was a part of the deal. You don't live your life as a part of the Deriugina School. You are a part of The National Team of Ukraine; you get paid and must do your best. We were the best in the country; we had to come every day with a smile and work hard. It is the School of Survival and Discipline. Do you have a few ounces of excessive weight? Jump until you lose it.

I felt like an engine there: start on January 3rd and work until December 28th in a dead run. There was no right to get sick, tired, or weak. If it was too harsh for somebody, they were free to go. Nobody was forced to stay.

CHAPTER 16

HOME GROUND

The gym of the Deriugina School, where I spent my early years, is located in the heart of the capital city on Instytutska Street 1 in the International Center of Culture and Arts of the Ukrainian Trade Union. It is widely known as The October Palace. It is a monument of architecture built in 1842, and today it is one of the biggest venues in Kyiv. Right next to the gym, there was a movie theater in the mid-90s; our team used to come to watch movies there. But unfortunately, after the Revolution of Dignity, the theater was damaged.

The October Palace is an old building. When we stayed there, the rooms were in poor condition, with many building cracks or fallen plaster. Despite this, our gym was legendary. Many generations of great gymnasts trained within these walls. It is a forge of Olympic champions. Iryna Deriugina herself started her career here.

The gym of the Deriugina School became every gymnast's home. We were spending here almost all our time from dawn to dusk. When we entered the school, we would go downstairs to the basement. Then, to a long passage with pictures of all the students on the walls. There was a glassy stand at the entrance with Iryna Deriugina and Albina Deriugina's trophies. It always made an impression on guests and looked like a museum.

At the end of the passage, there was a person on duty. It was impossible to pass undetected. She would tell the coach if you didn't say "hi" to her in the morning or "bye" in the evening. And you would be punished for inappropriate behavior. The coaches believed the Olympic champion should be a good athlete and a polite and respectful person.

Our mornings were usually active. First, rushing to the changing rooms, we went past the accountant's office. Then, on the left was Albina Deriugina's office, a tiny room crammed with trophies and awards. It was even hard to see the walls: diplomas, artworks, and photos of Albina Deriugina, with some famous athletes and political figures hanging everywhere.

Iryna Deriugina's office was different; the atmosphere was more vibrant. The interior was modern and well furnished: a leather sofa, a glassy table, a wardrobe included leather elements, photos with students, and awards. I always dreamed of my photo standing there one day, too!

Next door was a prehistoric massage room with a Soviet Union's iron-glass cupboard, where there was practically nothing except a first-aid kit.

And finally – the changing room – our small private room. Two athletes shared one wooden locker. We left there our clothes, shoes, and bags. Then, in the mornings, we all went upstairs to the gym, waiting for Albina Deriugina, forming a line. She was well-known for being very punctual. For instance, if the training session started at 8:30 a.m., the coach was already there by 8:10 a.m.

Albina Deriugina adored her job. She was a workaholic, literally living at the school. From the gym, we often heard her footsteps. While she was coming upstairs, we had 5-6 seconds to take a final breath before attacking the sports fortress. When the coach entered the gym, we stood in one line, keeping ropes on our shoulders. No jokes, no words. The start of the training was traditionally hard.

The main hall where we practiced with music was smaller than it had to be according to the international gymnastics' standards. It could not place two standard-sized training areas. The Ukrainian Rhythmic Gymnastics National Team has trained on inadequate training floors for decades.

The regular carpet size equals 45.93ft x 45.93ft (14m x 14m), and the working area is 42.65ft x 42.65ft (13m x 13m). We needed the whole line. The athletes needed more space to practice their programs appropriately. We had to come up with some lifehacks all the time. It was a huge problem. Because of the conditions we trained in, in real competition, stepping on the standard-sized carpet, the routine would crack. Size matter; It feels different, and you realize you don't reach the line; you are not used to the carpet size. Adjusting was always a real challenge for us.

In our gym, the second carpet was also smaller. While the coach was working with one of the gymnasts on the main mat, the other ten had to practice their routines on the small one. We dramatically lacked space.

Iryna Deriugina used to assign her favorite 10-10 exercise. She adored everyone working hard. It felt like an anthill: many people worked hard in a small space. Finally, the one who honestly accomplished all the tasks walked up to the coach and passed the exam on facial expression. If you got a red face – well done! It means you worked hard. She loved the red look. After 10-10, I was always bright red.

Next to the training area, there was a small room with a piano inside. Previously, it was an orchestra pit. It was my favorite place. I used to come there to warm up or to stretch my muscles. It was enough for me to stand still for a couple of minutes. I cooled down immediately, so I had to do warming-up exercises again. I always tried to come to the gym earlier. I wanted to stretch to make my body softer for the Amerykanka. My legs felt like wood if I had no time to do that.

Stretching inside the Deriugina School on your own was forbidden. Of course, you could do it at home or after the training session. I needed extra stretching. So, if people couldn't find me in the gym, they knew where to look.

Sometimes, the orchestra room also served for what we called 'miraculous transformations.' For example, we could achieve red faces for Iryna Deriugina there with the help of blush and lipstick.

Of course, a couple of creative young ladies who didn't like hard work and often sought easier ways. It was like a show. At first, the girls pretended to work hard. They disappeared awhile and walked up to Iryna Deriugina to demonstrate the result. I got furious occasionally for training hard, but others did it without breaking a sweat.

I tried to convince myself to cheat and put makeup on like others, but I didn't take my chance. I knew why I was working.

As time went on, Iryna Deriugina became suspicious. The girls, usually quite lazy, came to her red-faced very often. Then she, together with Albina Deriugina, started to check their backs. First, the coaches asked the gymnasts to turn around and check if the leotard was wet. But the girls came up with a new idea. Besides lipstick and blush, they kept a bottle of water in the cache. They would wet their backs and heads. After this trick, they quickly gained the coaches' trust.

So, while some of us were creating cheating plans, I hid to do an extra warm-up. Sometimes high windowsills were my lifesavers. I could sit on them and stretch. But the coaches got angry when they saw it; they thought we could break the sills, so it was forbidden.

There was a balcony on the third floor. Before I arrived in Kyiv, junior gymnasts usually occupied the balcony. All gymnasts loved it there, hiding to fill out the diary or resting.

Now, I feel nostalgic while thinking about the October Palace. I experienced different life moments there: sometimes bitter, sometimes disappointing, sometimes brutal, sometimes unfair, occasionally exemplary, excellent, and fun.

What naughty children we were sometimes when Iryna and Albina Deriuginas went out for some competitions, and we stayed alone! We went hog wild! Using a joyful moment of freedom, we organized a small party of naughtiness: we played games, made faces, danced, and laughed. It was great fun, but unfortunately, very rarely.

Winter was the most dreadful for training. The gym was cold. From the end of November and three more months, we were freezing. The temperature was only a little higher inside than outside. The cold air was coming through window chinks. We taped them to endure winter somehow. The cold was unbearable, but we had to work on a new program. Sometimes we ended up training wearing gloves, hats, scarfs, body warmers, two pairs of socks, and two pairs of pants. Wearing those, any gymnast looked three times bigger, and training was harder.

The most challenging task was to work with clubs and a hoop. Clubs are heavy; it was impossible to do something with them when your hands were ice-cold. When I inhaled, I could see your breath vapor. It wasn't enjoyable! This situation needed to be improved as the heating was off for years. We talked about this problem everywhere, visited TV channels, led press conferences, and gave interviews. All in vain.

Sometimes on a long day, we tried to cheer the coaches and ourselves up. We would decorate the gym with balloons for International Women's Day. For St. Valentine's Day, we would put hearts on. In winter, we would carve paper snowflakes. The most beloved holiday was New Year's Eve. We were preparing for it in advance. Our team was creative: some girls worked on décor, and some could write poems.

Usually, by December 20th, our amateur artists would paint a Chinese Calendar animal. For example, they put a pig up with ribbons and a club in the Year of a Boar. This tradition existed before us. Despite the strict school policy of total focus on gymnastics, we were encouraged to create art. Quite the opposite, it made everybody happier. We tried to find inspiration and joy even in small things. We hankered after some warmth, coziness, and festive mood, even in our tough lives.

CHAPTER 17

THE MOTHER OF RHYTHMIC GYMNASTICS

I want to dedicate this chapter to a wonderful woman without whom the world, and I personally, would not discover the depth of Rhythmic Gymnastics.

Unfortunately, Albina Mykolaivna Deriugina passed away on March 29th, 2023. It was a great tragedy for our team and our country. However, even though she's not physically there, I, as one of her students, will carry her legacy and input throughout my life, and I will pass it on to future generations.

She knew gymnastics well. She was an incredibly insightful coach who could find the right approach for gymnasts of different ages: from children to adults.

Apart from that, Albina Mykolaivna had a big heart. No words can express my gratitude to her and her family.

She was a true mother, an absolute authority, a mental guide, and an example to follow. If it hadn't been for Albina Deriugina, I wouldn't have achieved that much in sports.

As a child, the Ukrainian National Team head coach noticed me among Crimean girls and followed my progress for a few years. Then, she invited me to her school. She promised my Mom to keep an eye on me. In professional terms, it meant she wouldn't cut me slack. She kept the promise. I have always been hardworking, but I could hardly bear the intensity of Albina Deriugina's training.

From the first day at the school, Albina Deriugina paid particular attention to me. While Iryna Deriugina had individual training sessions, Albina Mykolaivna didn't go out for lunch; she stayed to work with me.

Figure 11. Kyiv, 2013. The World Cup. With beloved Albina Mykolaivna

"Here is the plan: after a four-hour-long morning warm-up, you stay in the gym and work on your individual program, no rest for you," she used to tell me.

I would ask, "Do I have to work without a break? As far as I know, after the individual programs, there will be group training". The answer was short, "If you want to achieve something – no breaks!". I memorized those words well. Thank you, Albina Deriugina, for seeing something in me and making me exert myself, even without lunch breaks.

She was a role model. Anyone who visited the Deriugina School and watched how she worked was probably shocked. Any twenty-year-old man or woman would be jealous of the workaholism of that eighty-year-old lady. At 9:00 a.m., she always stood before dozens of young athletes. We would listen to her without moving; we felt she could scan any of us like an X-ray. She could feel our mood and inner thoughts; she remembered what we had done the day before and what we should concentrate on. She had a computer in her head.

Many say that Albina Deriugina used to overload gymnasts with complex and unnecessary physical activities. I have a different opinion. Her warm-ups are known all over the world. She could see the benefit of every exercise; she had an accurate picture of actions in her head. All activities had their purpose. That was a mystery of Albina Deriugina's genius.

Figure 12. Albina Deriugina is helping me through mental breakdown

She devoted all her life to Rhythmic Gymnastics; she embraced and transformed it. Nowadays, Albina Mykolaivna is the only person who knows precisely every rule of our sport. She witnessed the development of the first generation of gymnasts. Hundreds of students were lucky to train by her. So, it's no wonder she could provide you with an athlete's profile at a glance.

"If you want to fly high, you have to love what you do, cherish it, and admire it," she told us. She was true to her words: she would spend all day in the gym. Even when she did not feel good, she came to work that cured her.

Her devotion and work ethic is legendary. To win Albina Deriugina's respect was possible only through diligence. Albina

Deriugina changed me not only as an athlete but also as a person. I learned from her devotion and accuracy.

Since 2013 she has been picked up by her driver, mainly because of her age. Iryna Deriugina uttered pleadingly that the car had arrived. But it never worked. Albina Deriugina always stayed longer. Then, in an hour, a driver would come upstairs to take her. It seemed she was never tired.

Some situations impressed me. For example, when our National Team won a significant competition. The team got the first prize and rushed home with medals. Everyone, including athletes, doctors, and coaches, was happy but tired, dreaming of rest. Albina Deriugina, on the plane, was holding a notebook in her hands, creating a plan for what we should do to become stronger. When we asked if we could relax, the head coach replied, "I saw strong and weak points of my gymnasts and our rivals. We can't lose any minute; we have to work on a flawless result; it means my gymnasts have to exceed the strongest points of the competitors."

She was often compared to Valerii Lobanovskyi by the methods and style of work: rigid, rigorous, disciplined, and with a thorough plan for every training. Sometimes we didn't understand her: spending so much time being involved only in Rhythmic Gymnastics is enough to drive one crazy! But Albina Deriugina constantly repeated, "While standing on the podium, you may rejoice; you are a celebrity. However, immediately after you step down, you are nobody. So, let us get down to work."

She never allowed us to think about rest or to become spoilt by fame. "Have you made your choice on Rhythmic Gymnastics? Then work till you drop!"

The coach was able to read our thoughts. She could ask, "Don't you want to work out today? Or aren't you in the mood for it?" This talent of hers sometimes would scare me. Once in a while, she would act like a therapist in her office. If I needed to share some intimate thoughts, I came to her. She was always attentively listening to me. I could lean my head on her shoulder and cry.

She sincerely loved me for my diligence, accuracy, working hard, and obstinacy. What she hated was laziness. She loathed lies and compared them to theft. "The one who lies is the one who steals," she would say. Lying was taboo. She supported the idea of having an honest attitude toward your work. I agree with it too. I could relax or take it easy, but I understood that I cheated only myself. I had a clear consciousness when I did my best before the competition. But I felt like a fish out of the water if I did not do enough.

Albina Deriugina had a calm and diplomatic personality. She never provoked any argument and knew how to resolve a conflict; her experience and wisdom drove her. Without raising her voice, her words were clear to everyone.

We respected and were a little bit afraid of Albina Deriugina simultaneously. Losing her trust felt like a verdict. On the other hand, she appreciated honest, trustworthy, hardworking, and neat people. It was possible to negotiate with or apologize to Iryna Deriugina and win her forgiveness with a smile. Still, it was impossible to do so with Albina Deriugina. If she was angry with someone, the game was over.

She had her specific teaching methods. For instance, we were prohibited from taking food or water on a plane. Sometimes she appeared angry with a gymnast without any visible reason. I would become tense immediately if that happened and call my Mom, saying, "I don't understand; I do my best and work as hard as I have been working before, but she is still angry."

Mom would also get nervous. Later we realized that Albina Deriugina wanted us to be a better version of ourselves. That was her motivation. When a person is often praised, it is relaxing. Albina Deriugina believed discipline was necessary, severe conditions to toughen the athlete's character. She thought waking up anger and delight in a gymnast was essential. A strong personality is usually required for victory in international competitions. Raising a champion is not easy. Yet she did it well for generations.

Albina Deriugina taught me to fight until the end. We were climbing to the peak with her when I was far from the podium, but she didn't let me give up. What was the point of wasting her time with unknown Anna Rizatdinova, who took 18th place in the competition? But she didn't leave me; she was not ashamed to let 'a loser' represent her school. She didn't betray me once and didn't refuse to train me because of my imperfect body or unsustainable results. On the contrary, she believed in me like nobody else. Even more than my Mom.

Albina Deriugina adored my Mom, Crimea, and the Crimean people. So, she never doubted my upcoming success for a second. Even when my Mom came to her office, saying, "I guess it's not working out; Annie shows no results." The coach replied, "Trust me, she will succeed. We've been through worse. I never give easy tasks; this way is even more interesting." Her deep faith made us move forward.

Albina Deriugina got a great sense of humor. When she was in the mood, she told hilarious jokes, which caused belly laughs. However, her life wasn't easy at all.

Having experienced war as a child, she survived a hard time of the mid-20th century, went through post-war Soviet hunger, endured the loss of her father in the war, and put up with poor living conditions. But she liked dreaming; unlike others, she was not scared of big dreams. For instance, she wanted to become the best Rhythmic Gymnastics coach in the world. And most important, she remembered the golden rule since childhood: to make a dream come true, you have to work a lot and never give up even if it looks like you have no chance to succeed.

She told us a lot about World War II and her youth. She was not only a sports coach but also a mentor. I remember one story she shared about her past. Once young Albina was honored to give flowers from a Ukrainian delegation to Nikita Khrushchev at the Union parade of athletes on Red Square in Moscow as a student.

It was rehearsed in advance: from which side to walk up the grandstand and how to move. For the parade, the carpets covered the stairs. Having reached the top of the grandstand, Albina stumbled and fell wearing her new dress, sandals, and a wreath while keeping flowers in her hands. When she raised her head, she saw a pleasant smile from Semyon Budyonny. The cavalryman helped her get back on her feet.

Then, after fixing the wreath, she said "thank you" and smiled back; she ran forward to give flowers to the Khrushchev as if nothing happened. It was brave for Soviet time to greet a leader so fearlessly.

At that moment, she realized that whatever happens can be fixed if you keep your confidence. So I always keep this story in mind.

Albina Deriugina was a strong-willed and tough woman. She went through real war and multiple sports challenges and never gave up. She was a real fighter, the Hero of Ukraine. She and her students raised the national flag of Ukraine for many years. In tandem with her daughter, Iryna Deriugina, she prepared numerous champions. I saw how deeply everyone respected her. The most high-ranking officials bowed, seeing her. The ability to find a key for every heart is a great gift that she had. That was one of the main secrets to the success of Albina Deriugina.

Figure 13. I won a gold medal in the final for hoop in 2013.

CHAPTER 18

TORTURE

Twice a year, Albina Deriugina organized sports camps for us, one usually held in Alushta, Crimea, at the sports complex Spartak, and a winter camp took place in the west of Ukraine in Berehove. Every summer, when it was time to go to Alushta, I wanted to quit, get sick, or vanish.

The camps were an absolute torture for me. We attached a calendar to the wall and crossed every day that finally ended; that was how much we loathed those camps and wanted to leave.

We usually went to Alushta camp in July. There were many people: all the National Team athletes and girls from other cities like Simferopol, Dnipro, Lviv, and Kharkiv. Every school sent three or four of its best students. There was a particular plan for athletes from the National Team. Every gymnast was supposed to have a journal to note down insights and observations. In Alushta, we had a rigorous schedule with no minute to waste.

We had to wake up at 5:45 a.m., and at 6:15 a.m., we had to form a rank at the stadium. Being late was the death sentence. Warm-up would start at 6.20 a.m: we ran around the stadium four times. While running, we were half asleep, and only by finishing the fourth circle did our eyes open.

Then, we picked up our stuff and moved to an open-air gym. It sounds nice, but it was just some fenced area surrounded by wire mesh with a wooden floor, where it was easy to slip and get injured. There was no carpet. But the management didn't seem worried. It took years until the floor got carpeted.

It appeared that Albina Deriugina was creating unbearable conditions for us on purpose. Painful? Not comfortable? Too bad. Deal with it! The only upside of all that was spending time outdoors.

With Deriugina's counting, everyone would lie on the yoga mats unfolded on the curved wooden floor, wearing ankle weights and doing Amerykanka 24 or 32 times. In the morning, at 6:40 a.m., it was still cold. We wore pants, socks, knee pads, and elbow sleeves to avoid injury due to unappropriated floor covering. The training clothes became no longer wearable after the camp; everything went into the trash.

It took an hour and a half to finish Amerykanka, which wasn't too bad. In the Deriugina School, we trained for strenuous physical exercise, so floor routines were relatively easy, with no hurting muscles, joints, or ligaments. After, we skipped rope exercises for 30 minutes. We were allowed to wear shoes, so this routine was at least bearable. Then, straddle bunny hops over a bench side and various power exercises. I must admit that I hated those jumps, and every time we had to do them, I begged off, saying I needed to go to the restroom. It was the only time I 'cheated' and didn't do what I was supposed to. After, we went to the first weight check, and at 9:00 a.m., we had breakfast.

One day we marched to the canteen after the first training, which lasted from 6:00 a.m. till 9:00 a.m. Boys from the Ukrainian National Wrestling Team, who apparently slept well, walked out, sending smiles our way. They had energy; we didn't. Everyone was impressed by the fact that gymnasts worked that hard. We didn't like the camp because other athletes, after their training, could go to the beach. Unfortunately, we had no such luxury. All we did there was training.

After breakfast, we had a break for an hour. Later the second training started at the outdoor ground equipped with wall bars. The tricky part was that afternoon weather was hot, up to +86-90°F (+30-32 °C). At 2:00 p.m., the temperature could reach +100-104°F (+38-40°C). We were not allowed to wear baseball caps because they could interfere with doing exercises, so we wore bandannas. The iron wall bars became almost white-hot; looking at them was painful. We were doing power exercises and sit-ups under the blazing sun for an hour and a half with no shade to hide. Albina Deriugina was always with us, following each step with a stopwatch. It was just unbearable. I still shudder to think of those wall bars.

We used to wrap up hands to keep them uninjured. However, the overheated iron made the skin not just blistered but bleeding. Before going to Alushta, we already knew what was ahead of us, so we bought many plasters, gauze rolls, and gloves. Everyone was hanging on the iron bars with bandaged hands.

Afterward, we returned to the training area with a wooden floor and practiced our individual routines without music. It was so dull. Heat, sultriness, feeling like a boiled dumpling. Then, after finishing up with exercises, we went to the second weight check, lunch, and so desirable two-hour-long break.

The third training session began with a choreography lesson conducted by Valentina Heorhiivna, a choreographer from Dnipro, and Anatolii Dumanov, a very experienced choreographer from Odesa. The class lasted for one hour and a half.

Then, Albina Deriugina gave us exercises on developing jumping skills, and we performed them on a wooden surface. What a "pleasure" that was! If someone scrunched a face demonstrating displeasure, the coach would say, "What about the past, when the gymnasts only trained on the wooden surface? Nobody complained!"

After the choreography class, we performed individual programs again, and at 6:00 p.m., we had to complete a ten-circle run. After the run, we could barely walk to the third weight check. Dinner was for those who deserved it - If a gymnast put on weight, she wasn't allowed to eat dinner.

We had an austere diet: porridge, soup, salad, chicken – low-calorie food. So naturally, we wanted to eat something forbidden. Some found a way to bring chocolate or candy bars, and some tried to buy sweets in town. Some girls escaped to the beach to treat themselves to cream horns or baklava. Wrongdoers were usually caught and punished. Albina Deriugina sent coaches to check rooms, fridges, and bags if somebody put on weight. In most cases, 'contraband goods' were found, and so was the 'smuggler.'

To lose some extra weight, we used a lot of tricks. For example, we wrapped our legs with cling film and wore compression stockings. That helped. Then, no one thought of the harm we caused to our health.

We were never allowed to go to the sea even though a beach was a ten-minute-walk-away. But frankly speaking, we had little desire to swim. We just dreamt of entering a room, loping down, stretching our legs, and resting. Sometimes Albina Deriugina took us to the stadium to practice with apparatus when it was hot outside. It looked like she did it intentionally. Sometimes I could not see the apparatus because of the dazzling sun, but I desperately tried to maneuver it.

I remember there was a tap for watering a lawn. And I intentionally threw a hoop or a ball in that direction to take some water and sprinkle my face with it.

What I used to detest was a cross-country run. We wanted to run to music to have at least some motivation. But, unfortunately, Albina Deriugina strictly prohibited this initiative. So, we had to hide our earphones under bandanas. Running around the stadium, we tried running up to sprinklers that irrigated a football pitch to get wet and cool. But, of course, that was also not permitted. It was impossible to cheat while running; coaches counted every circle.

I remember a horrible day when four individual performers, including me, got punished for doing exercises incorrectly on the wall bars. I would question it, of course. But who would listen to me?! It was the first and the last time I managed to run 20 circles around the stadium. Some girls stopped, some fell, and some refused to continue. I rued the day I was born but didn't give up. The world was going dark before my eyes. Then I noticed my Mom sitting on the chair and counting those never-ending circles. She was working as a coach there, too.

When I couldn't bear running anymore, I vented, "I hate you for making me do Rhythmic Gymnastics"! Mom often recalls it. Yet, I finished the run. I was so exhausted that I couldn't even cry. Stunned, I sat down on the grass and closed my eyes. I felt I would not be able to stand again.

We had only one massage therapist for the whole team of 30 people. Once in a while, it was possible to go to massage. Unfortunately, my muscles couldn't recover. They were so tight that sometimes I couldn't walk up or downstairs. I could not feel my body. When my parents came from Simferopol to see me, I cried on my Dad's shoulder. All activities were complex for me: cross-country runs, wall bars, and Amerykanka at 6:00 a.m.

After those ten days of camp, we were well-prepared even for a space mission. Of course, Albina Deriugina established the camps to strengthen and condition our bodies. Flexibility and strength don't go well together, but both are equally necessary for a successful gymnastics career: The camps helped to prevent injuries. We all had a good strength and endurance base for half a year. Then we had a winter camp.

This way, we used to keep fit throughout the year. Later on, I understood how vital those camps were. All I lacked was the most excellent physical shape and endurance, and all I gained there. After Alushta, 7-5-4-2 seemed easy. I did it without gasping or feeling uncomfortable.

CHAPTER 19

ALWAYS ROOM FOR A HOLIDAY

I'll share a secret: professional athletes dream of a holiday as a miracle. They are very similar to kids when it comes to holidays. There are almost no days off for gymnasts: no International Women's Day, no Easter, and no other public holidays during which all people rest and celebrate. New Year's rush is the only time we can relax, but only for up to 4 days. So we could go home on the 29th or 30th of December. But on January 3rd, we had to return to Kyiv. Being late would cause trouble.

Imagine you live in the same place, walk the same path, and follow the same rules daily: one false move, and you earn punishment. You have only one day a week to devote time to yourself and not really to yourself, primarily to household chores. And if you still have energy, you might go out somewhere. You don't even know how ordinary people live. You don't notice the change of seasons or see how flowers bloom or snow falls. If you are lucky, you may glimpse it from the train window on your way to the gym.

All your life happens in the gym with two coaches you know better than your parents. You feel their mood at a glance and understand what they want from you.

But people are not robots. There was a place for fun in our lives, too. We created that fun. First of all, we celebrated birthdays. When we were teenagers, we gathered in someone's house or the dormitory, in the birthday girl's room. Then, we played our favorite game: parodying everyone in the October Palace, impersonating Iryna Deriugina, Albina Deriugina, and Ireesha Blohina. Next, we performed sketches named "The Detestable Executive Committee."

We were aware of all aspects of coaches' execution methods and made fun of them. Then, we wrote speeches using coaches' favorite words and phrases and performed stand-up concerts where everyone laughed. We loved it; it was so much fun.

I had shared one room in the boarding school with Viktoria Mazur for three years. I was fortunate to have an optimistic and sincere roommate. Excellent and funny jokes were her specialty. She always managed to make a joke about everything. She used to cheer us up. She knew me very well and could predict my behavior in advance. When I won competitions, I was over the moon, got tons of greeting messages from followers, and spent nights reading texts from fans. But when I failed, I was down in the dumps, and Vika started to tease me, saying, "Oh, my poor girl, does nobody text you on social media? What a disaster." And for some reason, I would burst into laughter. We used to make some funny videos and tease each other. I have a lot of photos with Vika from those times saved on my smartphone. When I watch it again, I always smile.

Sports life itself imposed a rule; there are no friends in sports. Everyone fights by themselves for their place in the sun. Initially, I was apprehensive about that, but Dad calmed me down and explained that it's doubtful to be friends with your medal rival. Nevertheless, it bothered me deeply. I didn't let anybody close to my heart and couldn't be intimate with others. Although despite these "dog eat dog" rules, our relationships with Vika were warm.

We came to the Deriugina School from the outskirts of Ukraine. We were 15-16 years old but still felt like kids. Still, the best entertainment for us was a stroll in the shopping mall Globus. I was from Crimea, and Vika was from Luhansk. For us small-town girls, Kyiv seemed miraculous, a dream city from a fairytale. So we wandered the Globus mall, staring at colorful shop windows and eating ice cream in a café. When we finished, we went to buy chewing sweets from Candyland. We were stunned by everything. We were so excited to choose sweets, weigh them, and rush to the cinema with all those gummy treasures. It was a genuine pleasure to watch a movie and eat sweets!

Another joyful day was when Ireesha came over with her dog Lilu. We used to play a lot with that dog. I adored Lilu. Sometimes after performing 7-5-4-2 during the third or fourth repetition of the second apparatus routine, I would fall on the ground and refuse to get back on my feet. Then Lilu would run up to me and try to raise me with its little nose. I was lying on the floor, wiped out, with the dog jumping on my back, barking, and licking my face, neck, and hands. My mood would instantly change. I would stop crying, rise, and go to repeat the routine. Everyone loved Lilu. We called her a vitamin for our team.

From time to time, someone would organize a group going out event. Iryna Deriugina booked concert or cinema tickets to distract us from our everyday routine and expand our mindset. After Michael Jackson's death, we went to the theater Kinopalats to watch "This Is It." I will never forget that day! I was so impressed by his life story that I repeatedly replayed every song and dance move Michael Jackson created in my head. I wanted to resemble his genius.

In 2013 Ireesha Blohina took me in hand and often proposed to keep her company at various concerts. The wind of change had suddenly entered my life. We went to The Killers, Hurts, the Muse concerts a few times, and Okean Elzy.

When I saw Nick Vujicic, an Australian writer and motivational speaker born with tetra-amelia syndrome, a rare disorder characterized by the absence of arms and legs, I had an emotional explosion. He came to Kyiv in 2015 and delivered a speech in NSK Olimpiejsky. His life story turned my world upside down. First, I realized that our lives consist of complaints; we always grumble about circumstances, coaches, and exhaustion. But here he was, a smiley, optimistic, courageous man who had lived without arms and legs since birth.

I felt embarrassed. I thought of myself as an ungrateful thing that takes everything for granted. Yet, right then, the great desire to work hard woke up inside of me. And later, in some painful circumstances, I recapped Nick's story and didn't allow myself to give up.

Iryna Deriugina's, Albina Deriugina's, and Ireesha's birthdays were exceptional occasions for us. We usually made a lot of fuss over it, because developing an idea for a present was hard. Pictures, vases, and icons are old hats. So, we used to scratch heads over the unique greeting. One time we made a massive heart of red roses on the snow; our fingers were almost frozen, but we wanted to get noticed. Another time we came to Iryna Deriugina's house before the training and placed greeting posters and rainbow balloons on the walls of her floor. Once, we even ordered a cake to match her pistachio-colored car Audi TT with a signature on the car hood: "Happy birthday to the best coach ever!"

For Albina Deriugina, we bought a parrot, so she could have somebody to speak to at home. She laughed but seemed to like this gift. By the way, Albina Deriugina adored eating ice cream, so we bought a small fridge jam-packed with vanilla ice cream. The fridge later found its place in her office.

In 2012 Ireesha Blohina was a TV presenter of The Big Football on the Ukraine channel. People still remember her as a host who wore a yellow-blue dress with the same symbols on it as on the uniform of our football players. We ordered for her birthday a Barbie doll wearing the same dress. We placed the beauty on her car's hood and left flowers and a CD with video greetings from us.

We used to record and edit many greeting videos, and we wrote poems as well. We tried to create something unique every time, demonstrating our creativity and revealing something new in ourselves. It brought us great satisfaction.

After every big competition, there were organized parties, and we used to party hard! Usually, such events take place in beautiful restaurants. At the end of the dinner, when everyone finished their meals and drank some alcohol (except the gymnasts), someone always turned on the music and gave us full rein to hit the dance floor. We loved dancing. It was like a nightclub where we could release emotional build-up.

Typical young people at 17 usually spend time in entertainment centers and parks, have a private life, and have fun with friends in clubs. Of course, athletes are humans as well. We like holidays and parties. But for a gymnast, any vacation is taboo.

My family had a tradition of going together on vacation at least once a year. After the World Championship, Mom and Dad came to Kyiv to ask for my leave to go on holiday. And Albina Deriugina said the words I memorized once and for all, "You may take Annie away now, but when you get her back, don't be mad at me. After a week of doing nothing, she will develop a great rollback in progress, ten steps back."

And, of course, I didn't go. From 2010 to 2017, I had not gone on vacations. Hard work from January 3rd until 28-29 December without any breaks became my reality. Even following this schedule, some girls found time for love, friends, dances in nightclubs, and karaoke. For me, night live was odd then, and it still is. Perhaps I came to Kyiv having a rigid perspective. No fun; my aim is sport and nothing else.

So, I hid from the world and established a framework I created. I got to a nightclub for the first time when I was 20. I wouldn't say I liked attending birthday parties in cafes. I always remembered Dad's words, "Trips, parties, clubs, and fun won't escape from you. They will always be available. But Rhythmic Gymnastics is not forever; it will end very soon, and you will have a chance to live your life to the fullest."

I realize that he was right. But gym isolation also had negative moments: I didn't know what the real world looked like, I didn't have hobbies or friends, and I concentrated only on my goal. Due to that, I often suffered from nervous breakdowns. If you ask me if I regret it, I will answer no. The result of this voluntary sacrifice is the Olympic medal in Rio. It means I chose right.

But I don't encourage you to follow my path. We all are different, and every one of us has a mission. So my advice for parents who bring their children into Rhythmic Gymnastics is: if you want to achieve a lot, explain to your child that up to 25 years old, they will have to sacrifice the sweets of life, devote themselves to sport, be head over heels in love with it, to be an ascetic or a psycho who renounces worldly pleasures.

CHAPTER 20

LONG-AWAITED 27 POINTS

I want to share one of my journal records. I started journaling when I arrived in Kyiv on June 9th, 2010.

"Tomorrow, we are leaving for the Austrian Grand Prix. I am confident in myself, but my greatest desire is to do a new hoop routine perfectly." I wrote it about a very unusual routine preparation.

By then, I had been looking for my style for a while. Every individual performer must be unique and noticeable on the stage. Our ideas changed from one extreme to another: from Swan Lake to Hopak. But that time, we decided to take risks. We opted for heavy rock. This music is specific and not for everyone. We were unsure whether this style would blend in with such a delicate girl like I was. Would it create a look of harmony? I feared this change and didn't even have time to assess if I liked it.

The main point for me was building relationships with Iryna Deriugina. The coach became inspired by breaking stereotypes and presenting Rhythmic Gymnastics from a new perspective. So we opted for absolutely new movements and elements for this routine. I even became angry sometimes. I knew a set of complicated moves, and we surely knew what the judges thought of them. But Iryna Deriugina strived to change everything. As a result, the routine stood out from the rest.

Iryna Deriugina was so excited that she even remained in the gym after the training to brush up on the program. It was already dark outside, but we were polishing the hoop routine. Step by step, she made me do new moves well. She put every finger in the correct position and changed every transition, every head movement, and sight. It was not enough to be just expressive. Every breath in and breath out was vital. The girls used to make fun of it, saying it would take forever if Rizatdinova stepped on the central carpet with a hoop. Instead, the coach demanded I perform to the best of my abilities.

Iryna Deriugina created the idea of a brown-turquoise costume and decorated it with crystals herself. I was thrilled. Everything was going to change very soon! That was an excellent time for our friendly relationships; my triumphs were coming.

The aspirations were grand. At that moment, a new person was born, another me. Before that, I performed lyrical or fun routines. Mustering a rock for a mouse like me was challenging; nobody knew how the world would react. I was worried. There was further feedback on my new style; some were fascinated, and some disapproved.

My only wish for that competition was to do a new hoop routine without mistakes. But there were racing thoughts in my head, and I was trying to get rid of them by writing them down in my journal.

"I have to impress everyone. I want everyone to talk about me. I want to cause a sensation. I hanker for performing in the final! And finally scoring 27 points."

I concentrated only on that score. Only 27 points or more could allow me to get into the final. But, unfortunately, my dream didn't come true. Instead, I was eleventh. I performed my routines well, without serious mistakes, but it wasn't enough to get 27 points.

It caused me deep disappointment. I was shocked and devastated. We did all we could to change my style, add new elements to the program, and improve emotional expression, which didn't work. Then, being in a stupor, I went over my journal.

"I have to get first places to make big money for my coaches and me, and I will make it because I want it. Thank you, God, for everything you do for me. This competition has to be a turning point. I will earn everyone's respect. Everyone will like me."

This record reflects what was going on in my soul, my genuine dream to gain Iryna Deriugina's and all the gymnastics world's appreciation. Unfortunately, in 2010, only my Mom and Albina Deriugina were on my side. But I have to credit Iryna Deriugina: having seen no significant potential in me, she worked with me a lot then and was looking for a new style. But, eventually, there was disappointment again.

After Grand Prix in Austria, I approached our judge Lidia Vynogradna. I asked why didn't I get into any of the finals since I did all four routines without any mistakes. I couldn't assess myself correctly, but I wanted to know what I lacked. I had been slogging away at myself, all in vain; the door to the top 10 was still unavailable. The judge responded with a trivial phrase, "To get into Rhythmic Gymnastics top, you have to work harder and better." I understood that she didn't have an answer to my question.

Naturally, the Rhythmic Gymnastics world is tricky. It is tough to get into, but if you already became one of the best in this sport, all doors are open for you, and the world is your oyster. If you didn't get inside, then you may spend years taking from the tenth to the twentieth place because judges have a specific scheme of the best eight gymnasts in their heads. Getting into it is challenging because there are Rhythmic Gymnastics experts who are ready for the second Olympic cycle. You have to make a breakthrough! It would be best to have something unique, the cherry on the cake. I didn't have it.

Yes, I was good at pirouettes, but other gymnasts were also good. Apart from this, I didn't stand out, so the judges were not impressed. In 2010-2011 there were a lot of strong gymnasts in the world. It was even hard to get into the top 24. Why did I think I was destined to become the chosen one? The answer was obvious. My skills needed to be more advanced.

But I continued to fight. Sometimes I gave up. I worked at full stretch in the gym, the coaches praised me for being hardworking, and I enjoyed the sport, but every time there was a competition, I failed! Naturally, I was not too fond of it and started to doubt my choice occasionally. "Perhaps I do it all wrong. Maybe it's time to switch to something else before it's too late?" I thought. In moments of despair, my parents were by my side. Mom and Dad believed in my success and never let me give up.

I had extremely high ambitions then. But, indeed, I still needed to learn how to transition to another level. Still, I portrayed myself as one of the world-class Rhythmic Gymnastics athletes. It was my goal, and I was moving toward it. However, before Rio, my behavior was more modest. As a result, in 2010-2011, I overestimated myself.

The next record in the journal I wrote in Austria: "My main task, for now, is to master all routines. I have to enhance my skills noticeably. I want to change beyond recognition. I will become a successful gymnast. My task is to attend the gym having an aim and a purpose. I have an aim worth working hard, even harder than everyone else."

At the end of August, I wrote, "Thank you for everything, including failures, because they make me stronger. Performing new routines will help me get 27 points because they are much more developed. I have to perform them perfectly without losing apparatus or making mistakes. I will be different. I will become one of the best. I'm begging God to help me find the right way. I want to bring Iryna Deriugina joy and make her happy. I believe in myself."

After that, I went to the World Championship in Nizhny Novgorod, Russia, under the third number. The team consisted of Alina Massimino and Natalia Godunov. And again, I was beyond the first ten. I took 17th place. One more failure in my box of 'achievements.' As a result, I was not chosen for the club World Championship Aeon Cup in Japan, which I had thought about since childhood!

I was stunned by the unusual gym decorations: all pink, the symbol of the competition Hello Kitty everywhere. Mom told me a lot about this contest. She used to bring posters and brochures for me. Every new sign included a photo of a previous year's winner. I cherished a far-fetched dream: to take one of the winning places in all-around events and to appear on the poster one day.

My dream came true. In 2012 in Japan, I became the second, and in 2013 appeared on the poster, demonstrating a beautiful smile. But in 2010, I was crying because of resentment and despair.

I was on the verge of an emotional breakdown. Everything looked hopeless. I let Iryna Deriugina down again. The coach decided who would participate in Aeon Cup, and it wasn't me. I realized that she didn't recognize a good gymnast in me. Thinking and analyzing caused me a fit of stress. Parents were trying to comfort me, explaining that the club Championship was not everything. Dad said, "Don't worry; your time is yet. You will have your chance."

CHAPTER 21

QUEEN OF THE ELEMENTS

It is not easy to open up about someone you have controversial feelings for, as I have towards Iryna Deriugina. Those feelings vary from black to white. Some memories of us still give me shivers. But now, it is more straightforward; emotions and waves slowed down. After some time has passed, you start looking at things differently. You start understanding the reasons for some actions, noticing various hues in the portrait of another person, and your own emotions gain much warmer tones.

Iryna Ivanivna Deriugina is the head coach of the Ukrainian National Rhythmic Gymnastics Team, and the vice-president of the Ukrainian Rhythmic Gymnastics Federation is vivid, forward, and striking. She is different from everyone else. She can beam wearing black. Hardworking, a maximalist, a real fighter. She became an absolute winner of the biggest International tournaments twice, in 1977 and 1979, having exceeded all Soviet athletes. No one before or after her managed to do the same. She broke into the world of Rhythmic Gymnastics like a lightning strike; hot-tempered, with refined gracefulness and expressive body movements, she conquered judge's appreciation and achieved the love of millions worldwide.

In Iryna Deriugina's presence, the back straightens itself. She charms both men and women. Her winning spirit is well known not only around us, her students, colleagues, politicians, business people, and government officials. Tiredness is powerless against her will. Iryna Deriugina is a conqueror. There is no task she can't do: her eyes are always on the prize. She conducted Deriugina Cups at the top level even when the war started in our country in 2014. She is an excellent manager.

Iryna Deriugina is known as "the Queen of the Elements." She might be called that by those who know her and those who saw her in tournaments. When my Mom watched Deriuga's performances on TV, she was inspired and fascinated by her excellence. Iryna knew how to evoke other people's emotions. She could give a raging storm of accurate, flawlessly performed movements with graceful ballet on the carpet. Every move was genuine. The ability to show feelings through performance is a natural gift, hard to teach. When Deriugina was a performing gymnast, she created her deep emotional routines alone.

Undoubtedly, I had been dreaming that Iryna Deriugina would become my coach one day. My dream came true, but our relationship had gone through a rough patch: through hardships to the stars. When I first met Iryna Deriugina, I thought, unlike everybody else, what an unusual woman she was. Beautiful, stylish, but at the same time strict and demanding; looks like a flower but could give bitter, offensive comments. She is so extraordinary that her personality simultaneously captivated and repelled me.

From the first days in the Deriugina School, I had been trying to get Iryna Deriugina's appreciation. I had been doing everything I could to attract her attention, earn her trust, and, making no secret of it, get her love. I had been doing my best, hoping to get on the main carpet where her coach's eye would notice me at least sometimes. I wanted so badly Iryna Deriugina to start working with me individually. Even 10-15 minutes daily would be enough for my inner confidence. I wanted her to see my professionalism. I believed that this would come. I had to work to win her.

Iryna Deriugina despised laziness. She always said, "Diligence is crucial for me." However, I witnessed many times when she invited striking, naturally gifted, but lazy children to the leading carpet and worked on their programs. Her words rarely matched her actions. Her weak point was her attachment to expressive, beautiful girls she thought were physically built for gymnastics. She couldn't resist a visually appealing image. The result of such a method speaks for itself, whether I like it or not.

For 30 years of coaching, Iryna Deriugina students have won 120 golden medals, 30 silver, and 30 bronze in the Rhythmic Gymnastics World Championships, the Olympic Games, and the World and European tournaments. The list includes Oleksandra Tymoshenko, Olympic champion in 1992; Oksana Skaldina, bronze Olympic medallist in 1992; Tamara Yerofeeva, World and Europe champion; Natalia Godunko, World and Europe champion; Anna Bessonova, two-time bronze Olympic medallist in 2004 and 2008. I can also include myself in this list, Anna Rizatdinova, bronze Olympic medalist in 2016 and a World champion in 2013.

Undoubtedly, Iryna Deriugina is a unique coach. All Ukrainian gymnasts' routines have a touch of her exceptional style. She has a creative personality and has been creating outstanding programs for decades. A performance creation process is her calling. She has been doing that since 1992, starting with Tymoshenko, Skaldina, and all gymnasts of the Ukrainian National Team. Group genius performances also belong to her.

Iryna Deriugina used to choose music, looks, and style for everyone. She decorated our costumes. Iryna Deriugina fancies sticking Swarovski crystals on leotards. Working with costumes is her hobby and calms her down. She can do it all night long: first, she creates a design with the crystal pattern, then hangs up a leotard in front of the eyes and checks it for a couple of days, just like an artist with his painting. Then, she can change something again before finally sticking crystals. A genuine creator!

Moreover, Iryna Deriugina is an educator. She not only trained us but also dedicated her time to our education. Working on a new program with athletes, she always asked, "Do you know who created your hoop routine music? What film or ballet is it from?." Until 2013, only instrumental music was allowed in Rhythmic Gymnastics; no lyrics.

Once, I performed my ball routine to a glorious Swan Lake by Tchaikovsky. I was very responsive to what the coach told me. When

I came home and watched different variations from this ballet, it helped me to expand my outlook, filled my inner life with beauty, and distracted me from my everyday sports routine. I watched the movie Gladiator a few times, the music from which was also used for my performance to feel the vibe and to play emotions better.

In the Deriugina School, being an artist was even more important than technical skills. All for Iryna Deriugina. She claimed that you have nothing to do without emotions and feelings in this sport. It is not Artistic Gymnastics, where judges value precise movements and athletic strength. In our sport, a body is a language we speak to the world from the carpet. We carry a particular image with our performance. People often come to our contests, like to the theatre or ballet.

Iryna Deriugina could demand to work on emotional expressivity all day, and Albina Deriugina brushed up on the technical aspect. That was the uniqueness of their tandem. Iryna Deriugina loves improvisation. She said, "You are smart. So, improvise. Please, do it! You are an artist on the carpet!" But this approach was challenging for me; we were different in it. I need to have a specific task with direct instructions. I can't invent something; it's not in my personality.

Carmen routine became a breakthrough for me and Iryna Deriugina. Working on this program, we found mutual understanding at last. We worked together in the gym, only she and I, and we grew closer. Usually, program creation was complex for me: I wouldn't say I liked the draft version and improvisations. The phrase "Will finish it later" would agitate me.

Carmen brought us together. We went through some torturous training. I worked day and night at full stretch, but apparently, everything was wrong. I often heard, "You don't move on rhythm, don't get into the groove, or show proper emotion!" Nevertheless, I liked the music and the routine itself. It looked like we had found the way, but the picture still needed to be complete. Later we understood what we had lacked; it was the lively energy of a Spanish countrywoman, her recklessness and passion. "You are too kind, too virtuous for Carmen," Iryna Deriugina joked. I realized that she was right. There was too much modesty in my character. Then, I tried to play eagerness, and we succeeded. The audience always liked this performance.

With Albina Deriugina, the training process was merely technical. In contrast, Iryna Deriugina worked profoundly on creativity. I adored it when she said, "Ladies, today we perform to different music." She put a small CD in. There were about 20-30 tracks: songs, melodies, and popular top hits, from classical to rock and pop, just for inspiration.

It was boring to do the same routine job for months. So many repetitions every day, and even Carmen might make you sick. The image fades, you don't hear the music beat, and everything seems monotonous. It is crucial to "awaken the routine" and to add new colors. Iryna Deriugina watched us moving to music and inspected our progress with various tunes as far as a body reacts to a melody or rhythm. I enjoyed a lot such kind of work. We called these experiments an act of creation. And precisely for an opportunity to create, I adored Iryna Deriugina.

She always came to the gym with her favorite Yorkshire Terrier, Tiffani, who had accompanied us to all possible contests. Later, she brought another dog, Biba Brigitte. We were getting ready for the coach's arrival. One of the younger girls monitored the street from a big window of the October Palace. When Iryna Deriugina's pistachio Audi appeared in the parking area, the girl cried, "She's coming!" and we started to pretend we were busy.

Despite being strict and highly demanding, Iryna Deriugina is kind, supportive, and motherly. She is a great cook. Sometimes, before a significant competition, when we worked without breaks, Iryna Deriugina brought homemade food: buckwheat, borshch, roast chicken, or turkey. But all those yummies were available only for her favorites or super skinny girls, not to me.

My feelings towards Iryna Ivanivna varied from love and gratitude to misunderstanding and resentment. Nowadays, I am very grateful to Iryna Deriugina for motivating me. But at that moment, horrible thoughts raged in my inner child's Universe. Rereading my journal, which I kept for many years, I understand how traumatized I was. Iryna Deriugina didn't have a clue about it. The thoughts in my consciousness were growing into low self-esteem that she unintentionally put in my head. Work ethics wasn't the most important for her. Appearance played a key role, as well as body shape. Preference was given not to workaholism but to the physique, which drove me up the walls.

Half of my journal I devoted to Iryna Deriugina. "God, please, make my legs longer to make Iryna Ivanivna like me," I wrote, or "I have to attract her attention. I need Iryna Deriugina to notice me." I was on the verge of having a mental breakdown. I was thinking only about how to get her appreciation. The worst punishment was her ignorance. I had a lot of it. When she scolded others, I also wanted to be scolded. I watched her trying to get the result from a lazy gymnast, which made me jealous. My situation was different: I was ready to give it all to work with the coach and become her favorite! After all my failed attempts, I wrote on October 5th, 2010, "I need my legs to become longer, but I don't know how to do it. It is vital for me. Please."

I saw how Iryna Deriugina looked at other girls, how much time she devoted to them, and how excited she was when they succeeded. Even when she praised me, I didn't believe her honesty. I felt ignored; it was unfair. "She is doing that to stimulate other athletes," I thought. Initially, I called my parents excitedly to say, "Mom, I was praised by Iryna Deriugina! Can you believe it?". Later, I just said nothing. All those compliments seemed fake to me.

Finally, Iryna Deriugina gave me credit. It happened later, though, before the Olympic Games in Rio. At the time, her daughter Ireesha Blohina became my inspiration and support. Right now, I am grateful. Iryna Deriugina taught me to fight and believe in myself despite incredible difficulties, resentment, and misunderstanding. Our confrontation only helped my fighting spirit to become stronger.

Looking back at myself today, I realize I had good proportions. Yes, I admit, I didn't have legs like other girls, but they were not short. A lot of attention was paid to this, which wasn't right. I'm afraid I must disagree with Iryna Deriugina; the problem was not in my legs. I wasn't vivid, expressive, or memorable enough, but my legs were fine. Nowadays, the Rhythmic Gymnastics sport proves that height or weight does not matter. Different things are valued. It was absurd in my childhood; there were requirements for legs' length, a hip width. After competing in the Olympics twice and ending my sports career, I learned that nowadays, Iryna Deriugina is choosing girls by different criteria. She chooses willpower and hard work. It is impossible to climb high without these two, no matter how long your legs are.

Figure 14. LA, 2010. After the contest with our coaches Iryna Deriugina and Marina Kardash

CHAPTER 22

UNTYING KNOTS

In 2011, we attended the World Rhythmic Gymnastics Championships in Montpellier, France. It was the first qualifying event for the 2012 Olympics in London. Something unusual happened to me there while I was performing a ribbon routine. Before every performance, I checked my ribbon to avoid tangling incidents. What could possibly go wrong? After stepping on the carpet, I couldn't unfold the ribbon for the first time. I usually handled my apparatus with care, but I needed more experience. As a result, the day before, I folded my ribbon like I had never done before. I can't explain why I did it.

Anyway, I kept unfolding the ribbon, and somehow it magically tangled. There were seven knots! When I untied the first, the second appeared, the third, etc. Such a cycle of knots! The audience watched every move I made. It was a disaster. I just wanted the ground to open up and swallow me. My hands were shaking, and it made the situation worse. I tried to exchange that unlucky ribbon for a spare one, but unfortunately, none were left. I had no choice; I had to untie those untying knots. Time was running out. Even the audience started to cheer me up with applause. Everyone was shocked: the coach, the audience, and the judges. It was hard to describe what I felt then; it was painful.

Later, everyone in the Rhythmic Gymnastics world discussed that incident. Still, even now, the judges use it for their training. My case is rare and unexpected, unlike an apparatus out of the carpet, which always happens. The judges were confused; they didn't know how to penalize me for a performance delay. Nothing like that has ever happened in Rhythmic Gymnastics history before. I hope no one will ever be in my place with unusual accidents on the carpet.

After two minutes, I untied all the knots and started performing my routine without serious mistakes. But it was evident that I couldn't score high. After leaving the carpet, I went backstage, sat on the cold surface behind a curtain, and burst into tears. Albina Deriugina walked up and tried to comfort me. It did not help. I realized it was the end of my dream! I did screw up my chance of getting the Olympic license. All I had to do was repeat my routines perfectly well, which I practiced numerous times in the gym, but I failed. On top of that, I embarrassed myself before the judges.

I felt like I was dying. Again, another failure and no way out. I thought it was the end of my career. I didn't even get the license for the National Team, and Ukraine had always taken leading positions. I was overwhelmed with guilt.

However, in Kyiv, I got good news. In four months, in January 2012, the Pre-Olympic games took place in London. It was necessary to get into the top-6 to obtain a personal license. It was my second chance. When I learned about it, I understood God made me a gift and put it into a hard-to-open box. I had to make an effort to unwrap it.

Honestly, I wouldn't have gone to the Olympic Games in London if it hadn't been for this personal license. Viktoriia Shynkarenko would have gone instead of me. The coaches saw more potential in her, considering her to become a future star of Ukrainian Rhythmic Gymnastics. My box of achievements was a list of failures. So, I got lucky. My Dad always says, "Luck comes only to those who work." It may be a prize for my devotion.

Typically, the training process slows down after a big championship, but not for me. I had to try harder. I had to get a second wind. It was challenging to train in December when the festive mood was spreading around, and I only wanted to think about having a rest and seeing my family. But I dedicated myself to training. Even on New Year's Eve, I was training in the gym together with the girls. After the training, we went to celebrate.

We had to return to the gym on January 2nd. We had one day to rest. But I was in the gym already on January 1st. That morning I noticed I had gained 2 pounds during New Year's night. So, it was necessary to work to lose weight. So, on January 1st, when the city was celebrating, I was in the gym.

My persistence finally paid off. In January, in London, I received a personal license. I don't know what Iryna Deriugina felt then, but I was thrilled. I knew something from above was guiding me.

CHAPTER 23

MENTAL BREAKDOWN AND PAIN TEST

The year 2012 was exceptional as an Olympic year. Like an adult, I had to take things seriously, but I did not know any better. I don't think I prepared for my first Olympics as well as I could. I wasn't mature enough then. Sometimes, I was too laid-back at training and got lazy occasionally. As a teenager, I couldn't appreciate the rare chance I had to go to the Olympics.

As always, the Deriugina Cup was in Kyiv in March of that year. Before this competition, I had a ligament tear, and the old injury manifested itself. I had no intention of taking part in the contest. Finally, though, Albina Deriugina talked me into performing, "Annie, believe me, you won't feel any pain when adrenaline takes over." And she was right. Backstage, I almost couldn't move; I didn't warm up, and my foot hurt if I stepped on it. When I went on stage, the pain went away: I was performing leaps, jumps, and pirouettes as if nothing had happened.

After performing, the pain came back again. Nevertheless, the Deriugina Cup was successful; I took third place in all-around events, my first significant achievement in my home city. It wasn't an easy award, but I was proud. My confidence grew immediately.

Of course, I was not going to relax. Our team visited Minsk for the Grand Prix three months before the Olympics. The coaches wanted me to prepare hard for the most critical contest in my life with Albina Deriugina. The training process was unusual. We had a good training area of 13 x 13 in the International Exhibition Centre in the Livoberezhna district, which previously hosted Eurovision.

There were two carpets: one for practicing individual routines and the second for group ones.

Luckily, the Exhibition Centre was only two stops from the Lisova underground station, so I could spend less time on public transport. As I recall, in the group events, girls trained hard, but Alina Maksymenko and I often spent time arguing with the coach instead of working. Sometimes we would spend all day avoiding training.

Of course, such behavior affected the Olympics' results. The hardworking girls took fifth place in the group event and got close to medals. So, it became an indicator for me. I always knew that only one who works hard might achieve something, but I somehow forgot that notion three months before the Olympics. I was tense and did not know what to expect.

Young athletes' parents often ask me if I ever had experienced nervous breakdowns. Indeed, I have, and more than once. One of the toughest happened before the 2012 Olympic Games. Even the wisest Albina Deriugina didn't know how to deal with me. I ultimately refused to train. It was hard to believe: a hardworking girl, who always served as an example for others, could allow herself not to come to the training or show up and do nothing. To force or to talk me into training was impossible. Yelling, threats, and long conversations about the upcoming Olympic Games did not help.

Albina Deriugina tried everything she could and even invited my Dad to Kyiv. She was aware of our deep emotional bond. He was a motivator and an absolute authority for me since childhood. The coach believed it could help. When Dad arrived, he immediately assessed the situation as a military. Dad concluded that it wasn't just a whim, a joke, or an infatuation. He thought it was a nervous breakdown because of the extreme workload. Two years without a break, the World Championship, a difficult pre-Olympic week, and local competition in March with a ligament tear took its toll.

During that period, I didn't even have three days to rest. So, my body protested and decided to give up. My mental health couldn't cope with reality anymore. Even a professional athlete, being extremely perseverant, is not a robot. Rest is a vital part of a well-balanced life. Post-workout recovery is essential, and so is mental recharge. It's crucial to switch, to distract yourself from everyday routine: a cinema, books, TV shows, nature, and communication with friends. Changes help to grow. If you do the same things all the time, inspiration, motivation, and desire eventually leave you. Nothing brings joy when fatigue and void settle inside.

Dad tried to entertain and cheer me up. We tried to walk around the city more and visit beautiful places. We went a few times to the cinema. But, honestly, it didn't help a lot. When he left, my condition remained the same. I kept going to the gym without a particular desire to train.

Ireesha Blohina, Iryna Deriugina's daughter, entered my life right then. We hadn't been close before she started working for the school, just hi-and-bye relationships.

Once, Ireesha came and played different music at the training session. She had been living in the USA for a long time and got a great collection of pop songs. It was the first time I heard of Lana Del Rey. I instantly liked her music. I felt inspired again and went back to normal.

It looks like not a big deal, but different music brought new colors to my perspective. The preparation process remained challenging, but the crisis was finally over.

CHAPTER 24

MY FIRST OLYMPIC GAMES

Finally, we arrived in London. I was frightened when I found myself in the Olympic atmosphere and saw its greatness with my eyes. I wasn't ready and deeply regretted neglecting my training.

I clearly remember when we visited the Olympic gym a day before the performance. When the training started, I instantly felt paralyzed by fear. The coaches tried to help me out, but it was too late.

Looking back, I have to address young athletes. When you attend a competition, you must feel well-prepared and devoted and know you did everything you could in training. I learned this lesson the hard way after my first Olympic Games. After that, I always committed 100 percent to anything I was involved in.

In London, I needed more confidence. After finishing the training, we went back to the hotel. We already knew what the performance area be like, where the lights were, what color the carpet was, how many decorations there were, and what was in the background. Knowing this, the coaches had to decide what gymnasts would wear for the big day. Every girl brought eight costumes to Iryna Deriugina's room, where she had to make the final choice. During this process, she managed to piss me off, saying I was not ready. I left her room angry and devastated; and threw my leotards down on the floor of the narrow hotel corridor.

I was emotionally exhausted and screamed that I was leaving Rhythmic Gymnastics. I honestly believed that was the end. It looked like a nightmare. Other coaches collected my leotards and put them in my room. After this, Iryna Deriugina sent my Mom a message with a complaint, telling her about my obnoxious behavior and warning her that it would be my last competition. The second number of the Ukrainian National team was not allowed to behave this way.

Someone gave me my phone and showed me a text message from my Mom. The text immediately brought me to sense. Mom said, "Are you out of your mind? Stop talking like that! Listen to the coaches!"

After that, I felt like myself again, realizing it was too much. I was wrong and underprepared, but yet full of ambitions.

The following day the Olympics began. Albina Deriugina was always next to me. The first Olympic day was about the qualification round. I did my routines without serious mistakes, but my performance could have been better.

I remember waiting impatiently for the score. I could take eleventh or twelfth place, but only the top 10 gymnasts in the qualification round were to get to the final round. I was extremely nervous. I only had one thought, "I have to get into the top 10!"

Ireesha Blohina was the one who helped me to calm my emotions. Later she told me what I looked like at that moment, "We were sitting in the stands with Lida Vynohradna and Anna Bessonova. We watched performances and kept our fingers crossed. Then, after Annie's routine, Lida asked me what would happen if Annie won't get into the top 10?"

"And I saw it written all over the young athlete's face that her world started to fall apart. We will lose her if we don't bring her back to life right now. I felt her emotions distantly, and Lida seemed to read my mind. She told me to go to see Annie now."

"Everyone probably noticed my crazy eyes. I ran fast. When security staff saw my face, they let me into the area for coaches, athletes, and judges even though I didn't have a permit. I ran up to Annie, took her hand, and in a calming, fun way, said that she would get into the final because Ukrainian athletes always get in. But she didn't hear me. The girl was afraid; her world was on the verge of falling apart. Then I hugged her. Sitting beside her, I thought, why didn't anyone tell her there is a whole world outside Rhythmic Gymnastics? You are the world."

"Probably our faces looked so unusual that everyone wanted to film us. Stage directors were very interested in such emotions. They were filming us, not the leading athletes. I was staying as cool as possible, sure everything would be fine. Annie saw nothing; with a downcast look, she was thinking about her issues. And I told myself that when we arrived home, we had to start working on this girl; it was time to get rid of the blinkers on her eyes. Then I felt a connection between us. Everyone had already written her off, including herself. I knew I should take her under my wing."

It was the first emotional moment we got through together. When my result was finally up, and it became clear that I was the 10th, we could barely hold back tears. Even though, in my case, it was a success, I wanted to be better. I was full of energy and enthusiasm. I thought, "The 10th place is warm up. Tomorrow I will exceed myself; I will get into top-3."

Figure 15. Ireesha's crying

The second competition day began. I completed all routines, made a tiny mistake with the ribbon, and remained in 10th place. Ukrainian gymnasts always had leading positions or at least top-5. My tenth place meant a massive failure for the team.

It has been four years since I entered the Deriugina School in 2009. Everyone thought I was a consistent, hardworking, and diligent athlete. But I was so far from prize winners! The finalist of the Olympic Games sounded alright, but not to me. I always wanted more. I was dreaming of getting into the top 3.

After competing in the Olympic Games, I went to Crimea to see my parents. I felt terrible. At home, I announced that it would end my sports career. Years passed, and my stamina worsened, but there was no proper outcome. It all was for nothing.

More and more often, I thought, "What if Rhythmic Gymnastics is not my calling? Maybe I should start doing something else before it's too late?" My parents supported me. They saw how much effort, nerves, and health I put into it, but there was no result. Instead, the three of us sat in our home kitchen, thinking about what I could do after gymnastics.

CHAPTER 25

DEAD END

I kept my secrets in the diary. There I wrote all my hesitations, disappointment, and pain. The following record was made on August 28th, 2021, "Hard times have come. I need help. Lord, give me some advice. What should I do? I have doubts about whether I should continue my path in Rhythmic Gymnastics. It looks like a dead end. Am I going through a rough patch?"

"But I know this life phase has come to teach me. Life is giving me a lesson; sometimes, it punishes me. I may have to wait to overcome this. Maybe all is going to be fine. I hope so. I want to speak to Iryna Deriugina. What if things will change for the better? Though, I'm afraid Iryna Deriugina will ignore me until the competition in Japan. So, then we shall see. I have to live, enjoy, and appreciate every moment. Thank you, God, for allowing me to be involved in what I like. Thanks for the license, and thanks for the Olympic Games."

After a disappointing result at the Olympic Games, I wouldn't participate in Japan's club World Championship Aeon Cup. Still, I wanted to go. And right then, Ireesha Blohina miraculously appeared in my life again. For personal reasons, the girls who had to go to Japan couldn't make it. Ireesha Blohina, with Nina Yeresko, a coach from Lviv and my friend, vouched for me. Finally, they managed to talk Iryna Deriugina into it. They gave the following reasons, "Let Rizatdinova go for the last time."

The coach hesitated but finally gave up, considering the circumstances. I was over the moon! At least something nice happened to me in 2012. I was sure it was the final round of my athletic career. However, I wanted to end it on a positive note.

As I had anticipated after London, Iryna Deriugina was ignoring me. My inner child didn't allow me to apologize. Iryna Deriugina also didn't move toward me. I remember the prep before Japan. I had to train on my own. The coach didn't want to notice me; she only played my music, and I did two or three run-throughs. I would need feedback that I didn't receive. We existed in the gym like this until Japan. Although the preparation process was short, only a few weeks passed after London, and we went to Japan.

Every person goes through hard times sometimes: a creativity crisis, a midlife crisis, a love crisis, an existential crisis, etc. It's impossible to hold up well all the time. Sooner or later, our fate tells us to stop and think about what is happening. After the Olympic Games, my inner crisis became even worse. A misunderstanding with Iryna Deriugina didn't vanish into thin air. Moreover, due to many reasons, it even worsened.

Things like fatigue, the same conversation topics, a monotonous routine in the gym, and critique put too much pressure on me.

My whole life consisted of Rhythmic Gymnastics. I had no real friends, only teammates, so I stopped believing in friendship. My parents lived far. I deliberately cut off any attempts to have a private life, no movies, no dates. I was breathing Rhythmic Gymnastics. Perhaps it happened because Dad told me in childhood, "If you hide from the outer world and put every effort only in what you like, if you do your best in what you like, you will be successful."

I had been moving towards this since early childhood. Even as a teenager, I wasn't interested in boys or parties. I went to the nightclub for the first time when I was 20. Before that, I selflessly to the sport. I don't regret anything. However, if you ask me about emotional breakdowns, they happen because of physical, mental, and emotional fatigue. Every minute 17 hours per day, 365 days a year, every year was about Rhythmic Gymnastics only.

It's tough to live without entertainment or distraction. When there is no switch from one activity to another, it is damaging to mental health. After the training, I watched motivational movies about sports at home and wrote. Sometimes I felt like there was not enough air. I needed to figure out where to find at least a little bit of fresh air, where to find the power to move on because I knew I was obsessed.

After the Olympic Games in London, I reached a turning point in my life. I realized that I had been doing something for all that time and didn't know how to continue. It was like a disappointment in everything I knew and loved. And this time, Ireesha Blohina saved me again.

CHAPTER 26

LIGHT AT THE END OF THE TUNNEL

In October 2012, we attended the club World Championship Aeon Cup in Japan on behalf of the Deriugina School. Viktoria Mazur and I represented senior gymnasts, and Anastasiia Mulmina was junior. Again, I was on cloud nine. But I was done waiting for a miracle and treated the competition as the last in my career.

After the Olympic Games, it was common for athletes to leave the sport. Typically, this is how transfer from one generation to another happens. When the older gymnasts go, the young take their places and can make it to the next Olympic cycle in 4 years.

In Japan, we were to perform four routines: hoop, ball, clubs, and ribbon. I didn't set a goal to get into the top 3. I knew the best gymnasts always come to Japan. Therefore, I was okay with the idea that I might not get medals. In 2012 the Rhythmic Gymnastics elite at the Aeon Cup was represented by a silver medalist of the Olympic Games, Daria Dmitrieva from Russia, a bronze medalist Liubov Charkashyna from Belarus, and Aliya Garayeva from Azerbaijan, who became the fourth in London. Honestly, I had poor chances.

I knew I was about to end my career, but I cherished a dream of performing at the Aeon Cup. I was relaxed and decided to feel the moment. I walked to the carpet and returned with a smile, which wasn't typical for me.

Ireesha and I were already pretty close by then; we texted each other all the time. I remember very well how I got a message from her before my turn, "You are a diamond. Shine bright! Good luck! You can do it!" It was nice.

I became second after Daria Dmitrieva in all-around events. I texted first Ireesha and then my Mom. Nobody expected me to do that well, not even myself. Our team took third place, which was a good result for the school. The Russians were first; Belarus came second. I was overwhelmed to realize I was finally worthy.

Professional sport is about reputation. You may turn into a princess in a day or step down to Cinderella reasonably quickly. One failure, and you are out of the top 8. A ranking and reputation are among the most essential components of Rhythmic Gymnastics. In the twinkling of an eye, I turned from an ugly duckling into a beautiful swan. The judges finally noticed me, and the coaches wanted to train me.

Figure 16. Kyiv, 2013. The day before the Home Championship with Ireesha

I found a second wind. It felt like I started to write my life story from scratch.

Before that, I worked in the gym for long hours without encouragement, support, or appreciation. But It was necessary to go through such a dull phase. My journey wasn't easy. Sometimes I saw no light in front of me. At one point, I lost hope. Thanks to God, I didn't give up. I am also grateful that when I needed Ireesha the most, God sent her to me with his words coming from her, "You don't need to quit. It is a new beginning for you."

Not only my life changed. The rules for Rhythmic Gymnastics did, too. The changes happen every four years after the Olympics. It was my lucky chance. The judges started scoring pirouettes much higher, and I had always been good at it. Also, the gymnasts were encouraged to pay attention to the artistic part of their performances and add dance step combinations to their routines. I liked those changes. From my standpoint, it was absolute Rhythmic Gymnastics.

From that moment, everyone could earn their points: some with technical elements, some with charisma, some with pirouettes or apparatus handling. These rules were familiar to the Ukrainian school because our coaches always paid particular attention to emotional expressivity. As a result, there were more opportunities for us. Everyone on our team regained passion again!

CHAPTER 27

NEW ERA

The new era of Rhythmic Gymnastics has begun. We started spending even more time in the gym. Every athlete was allowed to pick out diverse music, from classical to the world's best-known songs. All was so unusual, interesting, and experimental. Before, coaches assigned the music piece. Ireesha Blohina also encouraged me to appreciate the changes that came.

After returning from Japan, we started to work on an exhibition performance for the Rhythmic All Stars Gala in Korea in November. We were impressed by Ireesha Blohina's unconventional training approach during the Olympics. She was a pioneer who brought a lot of American novelties to our Ukrainian world.

After discussing the music for an exhibition performance in Korea, without any hesitation, we decided on Summertime Sadness, the most popular song of my favorite singer. As I said earlier, Lana Del Ray and her music helped me to overcome an emotional breakdown before London. We uniquely approached my new routine.

One day we finished training late. On the way home, I was so excited about my new routine I couldn't stop thinking about it. It was late, so I took a train, where I had much time to think. I felt like a beautiful flower was blossoming inside me, like something new was coming into the world. So I took a smartphone and started texting "thank you" messages to Ireesha. I was grateful that she could connect with me. Our cooperation inspired me.

It was the best exhibition performance in my whole sports career. It sure was my favorite. In Korea, Ireesha creatively styled my hair. You could see her uniqueness in everything: the music she liked, the costumes she designed, her hairstyle, and her make-up. She said, "I notice someone's weak point and cure it. I select music that an athlete would never choose by herself, and with its help, I try to reveal the true meaning of Rhythmic Gymnastics. I invited a talented Crimean designer Ilyas Sahtara to make an innovative outfit for Annie's performance."

"I wanted to create a new Rizatdinova. I wanted her to be reborn, to forget what she had been before. In this exhibition performance, Annie revealed a new world in herself. She had no idea it existed. Like Annie, the song was shiny, feminine, romantic, and tender. I highlighted her eyes to make them more noticeable. Ilyas and I chose purple for a costume. People with closed upper chakras usually are indifferent to purple. They call it blue, light blue, or pink. I chose purple on purpose as it awakens consciousness."

Ireesha was right in her theories; my consciousness awakened. While performing, I became one with the song; I saw no light, no spectators. There was only a tender voice and me. Ireesha predicted how I would feel. Again, she revealed those hidden corners of my soul I knew nothing about. The audience was captivated by the performance.

Since then, a new stage in Rhythmic Gymnastics has started for me. I learned to be different. Generally speaking, making new programs was the most productive and pleasant from the end of 2012 until the beginning of 2013. Even cold winter did not bother me. Athletes usually put on weight in winter. It's hard to lose weight without heating when everyone trains in gloves. A body shivers because of the temperature. Winter in Ukraine is not suitable for art. But that time, it made us peppy.

The time to go to the winter camp in Berehove came. I bravely declared I was not going anywhere before finishing all four routines. So, Iryna Deriugina, Ireesha, and I stayed in Kyiv to work on my program. Ireesha took an active part in the process. We intensively worked together. First, what we got ready was a hoop routine to the famous Moonlight Sonata by Beethoven. It was Iryna Deriugina's idea to work with classical music. I wouldn't say I liked Beethoven's music, so I was against it. I couldn't imagine it would bring me a gold medal at the World Championship! But, sometimes, it's crucial to trust professionals.

To connect to Beethoven's Sonata, the school sent Nina Yeresko and me to Lviv. Nina took me to "the most expensive restaurant in Ukrainian Galicia." The place looked refined. The atmosphere, the dishes served, a flickering candle flame, and live music inspired me and took me away from everyday reality. We treated ourselves to some dry wine, even though I didn't drink alcohol then. We also asked a pianist to play the Moonlight Sonata. I felt enlightened. Suddenly I understood what the coaches wanted from me: I wasn't supposed to be a playful girl; I had to turn into a noble lady. After that beautiful evening in Lviv, I felt the music differently, and the routine became complete.

We picked out music from the movie Basic Instinct for my ball routine. Ireesha suggested for the clubs routine an exciting song Parov Stelar L'etoile. People called this song cosmic due to the exquisite saxophone tune. However, even though half of the audience disliked this music, the routine still found its fans. The performance was dollish, extravagant, and unique.

For my ribbon routine, we used the famous Mexican song Bésame Mucho. With Ireesha, we measured every step and worked on my choreographic skills. We made the performance dynamic. My emotions finally came through. I guess the expressivity always lived in me; before, I lacked the inspiration and imagination to access it. Finally, I began to reveal myself, to show my emotions through body movements, eyes, and smiles. There was no need to ask me to do it.

My new program was outstanding. It was the first time the Ukrainian National Team had an uplifting program, different from the usual dramatic style. Traditionally, there were gladiators, Troy, Armageddon, Pearl Harbor, the war, and drama. And now, we added a spark of happiness and joy.

I decided to stay in Rhythmic Gymnastics a little longer. I got interested in what was going to happen. I enjoyed the process and my new program! With Ireesha there, everything became different.

CHAPTER 28

TURNING POINT

At the beginning of 2013, a junior gymnast Eleonora Romanova and I went to the World Cup in Estonia. We went with Lidia Vynogradna, a Ukrainian judge of an international category. It was the first competition of the year, the trial one. Many athletes needed to adapt to the new rules and learn the specifics of dance step combinations. But, on the contrary, I was very well-prepared to win the World Cup. I got medals in the finals. Wow!

I told myself, "Do not be so happy just yet. The Russians aren't here yet". The news immediately spread all over the country. I became famous in one night. I won the gold medal in the World Championship in all-around events. The media was suddenly obsessed with me: interviews on the TV and radio, articles in the newspapers and magazines.

The following stages of the World Cups started. Contest by contest, I was getting results. In Portugal, I got a bronze medal in all-around events, two more silver medals, and one more bronze. In the World Cup in Pesaro, Italy, I got three awards in the finals: a hoop, clubs, and a ribbon. Two silver medals and one bronze I brought from Bulgaria. In the Grand Prix series in Corbeil-Essonnes, France, I won a gold medal in all-around events, a gold for a club's routine performed to cosmic music, and two more silver medals and one bronze in the finals.

Then I always came back home with medals from competitions. I was living a dream in 2013. The judges gave good scores, and I began to earn monetary prizes. I was thrilled to bits. But I told myself, "The main thing is not to slow down, to work even more, not to be lazy, not to feel superior." I knew the door had opened, but it could soon shut. I learned how it feels to knock behind the door for ages. So, after I had grasped it, I couldn't lose my grip. Finally, however, the Universe gave me a chance. With a clear conscience, I worked much harder in that period than in all previous years combined.

On June 2nd, 2013, we won a silver medal in the European Championship in a team with Viktoria Mazur and Alina Maksymenko. The following day I won a silver medal for the ribbon routine. It was my first medal for an individual event at the European Championships.

Then I went to Kazan for the Summer Universiade; it's like the Olympics held among students. We represented our university, the National University of Physical Education and Sport of Ukraine. It was my first time living in the Olympic Village, which differed from London, where I stayed in a hotel apart from the Ukrainian National Team. In London, we didn't have a chance to experience the Olympic vibe fully. But in Kazan, staying among the best athletes in the world, I felt connected to them all.

On July 15th, I won a bronze medal in all-around events. It has meant a lot since the Universiade took place in Russia. I didn't have much time before the next World Championship, and ending up on the medal stand was pretty challenging. On July 16th, my birthday, I got third place for hoop and ball routines and second for clubs.

I made a gift for myself and got three medals. One more exciting event happened this day. After my final ribbon routine in the massive Palace of Sports, I heard the Happy Birthday song. The fans gave me flowers and said beautiful birthday wishes. It was unforgettable. One of my favorite singers, Zemfira, performed at the Closing Ceremony.

Back in Kyiv, we only had a little time to rest. After that, we went to Colombia for the World Games. Yeromina Natalia was a judge representing Ukraine; she spent much time with us and evaluated our performances with other judges, Lidia Vynogradna and Yuliia Atrushkevych.

At the Olympic Games, Rhythmic Gymnastics has always been presented only in all-around events. In the Columbian city of Cali, we performed only in the finals. The authorities warned us about a dangerous criminal situation in the country. We were not allowed to go out alone. We had maximum security provided by the host. The weather conditions could have been better. Due to high humidity and heat, ribbon routines were called off, so we performed only three: a ball, a hoop, and clubs. I got a gold medal for a hoop, a silver one for clubs, and a ball.

Figure 17. Italy, Pesaro, 2013. With Ireesha Blohina and Iryna Deriugina.

Photo by Enrico Della Valle

After returning home, Alina Maksymenko and I received invitations from the Ukrainian Ministry of Sports, where we got a long-awaited title of "The Honoured Master of Sport of Ukraine," which equates to an international champion who has made valuable contributions to the sport at the highest rank possible. After that, I became a desirable guest at the City Council. The life I had always been dreaming of began.

On August 25th, 2013, I received the Order of Princess Olga of III degree award for the achievement of significant sports results at the XXVII World Summer Universiade in Kazan, displaying the dedication and the will to win, raising the international authority of Ukraine. After the Universiade and the World Games, I got prize money from the state and bought myself a condo in Kyiv. I was 20 years old, and everything seemed to be a miracle.

But I didn't relax. After every contest, the judges and I examined my cards. I used to contact Lidia Vynogradna and Yuliia Atrushkevych and ask them for professional help. The cards are printed forms, where is kept the record of all our routines. Judges always have them around to cross out or tick well-performed failed elements. Even when I won the World Cups, judges examined my routines and sent me feedback. They highlighted all I had to check out or work on.

Figure 18. Italy, Pesaro, 2016. After the contest with Iryna Deriugina, Ireesha and her little daughter Jackie and our judge Yuliia Atrushkevich.

In the beginning, my cards were all red with their marks. I even resented Lidia, who, not considering my accomplishments, would send a card full of red notes. She would thoroughly explain, "Look, you didn't earn points here. You didn't do pirouette properly; you didn't hold a move long enough or show the amplitude." Later I learned how hard she worked to help my coaches and me.

Sometimes Lidia even came to the gym, and we counted every step with her and Ireesha. We worked on correcting and adding new stuff to the routines during the year. Thanks to this, I was very well prepared for the World Championship. That time almost all elements on my card were spot on.

Our whole team, including coaches, was over-motivated because the Rhythmic Gymnastics World Championship 2013 was going to be in Kyiv. We trained non-stop. We knew that we had more chances to win at our home ground. In Ukraine, we say that the walls at home are your friends, your comfort, and your helping hands, meaning that the odds are in your favor when you feel local support. Our audience in Kyiv is the most supportive.

CHAPTER 29

HOME CHAMPIONSHIP

This preparation process for the World Championship was mentally and physically the toughest. At first, the coaches had differing views on the training approach. For instance, Albina Deriugina inclined her plan, 7-5-4-2, to achieve accuracy through numerous repetitions. On the other hand, Iryna Deriugina wanted us to do only two or three run-throughs but with complete devotion and expression. I supported Albina Deriugina.

The training was held in the Palace of Sports on the carpet for the upcoming competition. We followed Albina Deriugina's directions. Usually, after administrative meetings, Iryna Deriugina would show up, and here a fascinating part began. She disapproved of our work, and it caused arguments. I remembered the experience of my first Olympic Games and knew that two run-throughs were not enough for me. I liked repetitions because I saw the result.

Arguments, talks, and disagreements distracted me greatly. I also expressed my point of view, which made things worse. The training often was depressing. Thankfully, Albina Deriugina and Ireesha supported my vision. So, they decided that Albina Deriugina would prepare me while Iryna Deriugina would work with Alina Maksymenko.

Then we agreed on who would accompany me during the World championship. It wasn't enjoyable when the coaches tried to decide to whom I belonged. The number of arguments overwhelmed me. My Mom, an honored Ukrainian coach, was helping to get the girls ready for group events, so she witnessed the whole thing. I can't imagine how it felt for her.

Alvin's Deriugina assured my Mom that everything would be alright if such a coach covered up for me. This way, Alina Maksymenko and I got down to 7-5-4-2. And if before London, the coaches forced us to do it, this time we had enough enthusiasm and motivation. There was no need to push us anymore. We became older, mature, and understood what was necessary to do.

Anyway, we ended up having one more fight with Iryna Deriugina. It was so bad that we couldn't stay on the same ground together. Alina and I even got different schedules, which is atypical. First, Iryna Deriugina worked with Alina. Then, after that, they would leave, saying: "The training area is ready for the next gymnast." Albina Deriugina was responsible for music, and next to her was Ireesha, so they were working on getting me ready. That is what our preparation process looked like.

In the last two weeks before the competition, I didn't come across Iryna Deriugina. Needless to say, I was scared. The conflict with one of the leading coaches and the slightest mistake at the World Championship would mean leaving the National Team. Iryna Deriugina didn't fancy the idea that Albina Deriugina and Ireesha joined my preparation process. We sometimes had to move to another gym because I needed access to the training area or music, which I didn't have. It was hard to cope with. Sometimes I thought, "If I make a mistake, I fail. It will be the end." It was impossible to go against Iryna Deriugina.

Naturally, I was nervous and didn't understand how it would work. But it was a do-or-die situation; either I go and perform the program perfectly well, or I fail and say goodbye to professional sport. But I knew I was well-prepared, and knowing this comforted me. It was the first time in my life that I knew that I had done all I could. I felt courageous. All routines became nearly my subconscious self.

A few days before the competition, we stayed in the President Hotel, where athletes from other countries lived. I suddenly wanted to go outside on the final night before the contest. It seemed there was not enough fresh air to breathe. So, I went out. In the hotel yard,

I found a tree. I put on a hood to attract less attention. I sat under the tree, raised my head, and started talking to God. It wasn't like a traditional prayer. Instead, I communicated in my own words, 'God, you witnessed the challenging preparation process I went through. I honestly did all I had to. I worked until I dropped. Please help me to perform well."

My words were so genuine that I burst into tears and immediately felt better. After that night, I set a new ritual: before every important contest, I went outside, found myself in a dark corner of the park or by the sea, and talked to God. It calmed me down, raised my confidence, and empowered me.

Finally, the day of the competition came. The first medal was at stake. Albina Deriugina and Ireesha accompanied me. Alina was with Iryna Deriugina. Unfortunately, I performed under the first number in the first final, which could have been better for me because, in the beginning, judges usually try to take stock of a situation on the carpet and typically do not give athletes high points.

I did a hoop routine without mistakes. The audience encouraged me; I remember that unforgettable feeling when the whole country stood with me. I earned a good score. And I thought, what if those high points got me closer to the awards? I might even become the third. After hoop finals, I was changing clothes for a ball routine. Suddenly, Iryna Deriugina got a call from somebody.

Alina and I were on the same ground when we received news that I won. Iryna Deriugina was showing me with a finger "number one." I burst into tears, and so did Ireesha. Albina Deriugina was trying to bring us to our senses, saying, "Stop it, calm down! We have one more routine to show." But I stood still, held a ball, and thought, "God, I am the World Champion!" I was repeating it to myself and couldn't believe it. For me, the world champions were athletes like Anna Bessonova, Tamara Yerofeeva, Kateryna Serebrianska, and Olena Vitrychenko. I was so used to the role of an ugly duckling, constantly trying to earn Iryna Deriugina's loyalty and being a grey mouse who always ended up taking low places. Not anymore. I was the champion! Unbelievable! A year ago, I wanted to quit Rhythmic

Gymnastics. Instead, I raised my head and thanked God for such a miracle.

Then I started performing a ball routine in the successive final and made a mistake that prevented me from getting closer to a podium. Later I got a silver medal for a ribbon routine and another silver for all-around events. And naturally, the one for all-around events was much more valuable because it was an Olympic program.

But frankly speaking, only some people remember these medals. In Kyiv, my gold medal attracted the most attention. After Anna

Figure 19. Kyiv, 2013. I won a silver medal in Home Championship

Bessonova, it was the first time someone got it, so all of Ukraine got to know me. I started receiving many photoshoots proposals and event invitations; world-known coaches began to pay attention to me. I entered the world of the elite for which I had been fighting for the last five years. It was my triumph! There were tears of joy in my Mom's eyes.

However, only some were good. Something very frustrating happened in the Championship. Having spread on the internet, it attracted too much attention worldwide. An accident occurred during the podium ceremony: a Russian anthem was played instead of a Ukrainian due to technical issues. I started to sing along. It felt like it was not happening to me. I was in a euphoric state. Just imagine a twenty-year-old girl who just won after so many failures! My emotions at that moment were hard to express. I didn't only get into top-3; I was gold. Some journalists were happy to exploit the situation and made it nearly the most important event of the World Championship. The press craved scandal; it drove me crazy.

Standing on the podium, I was hypnotized, turned off completely. When the music was on, I began to sing something. I was staring at our flag and felt happy to be there. Then, I realized that the melody was wrong. I turned my head to the staff responsible for the music. They had already noticed the mistake and changed the CD. All spectators were singing the anthem of Ukraine along with me. But the main point was that Ukraine won its gold at this World championship. After that, however, the press crucified me. A year after Russia invaded Ukraine and annexed Crimea. The press used the story with the anthem many times.

But anyway, there was much more rejoicing. Longines, an official partner and a timekeeper for World Rhythmic Gymnastics championships, awarded me the prize "For elegance." I had been dreaming of it for a long time, watching how other athletes received it. And my dream came true! I felt incredibly joyful because I earned the award for my country in Kyiv, our capital. Longines Prize "For Elegance" was set up in 1997; it takes the form of a trophy representing a gymnast in movement. It was created for Longines by the Swiss artist Jean-Pierre Gerber. In addition, I received a Longines timepiece and a solid cheque.

I want to mention one of the most positive effects of this Championship – it brought a lot of limelight to our kind of sport. Before the contests began, L'Officiel released a new magazine edition with me, Ireesha, and Alina Maksymenko on the cover. We had a photo shoot in Vogue. There also appeared a massive poster with our pictures in the Arena City, from which we looked at Khreshchatyk, and all of Kyiv could see us. We attracted a lot of media attention. Posters with our pictures were even in the subway.

People were interested in the upcoming World consents. But unfortunately, in Ukraine, it is possible to attract some attention to sports only by organizing a massive event. The national sport is the face of the country. And I dream of sports becoming a state and social priority. Famous athletes who help raise the country's image through their victories must be recognized and respected by fellow citizens. We win for our country by sacrificing our time and health. The young generation should look up to athletes.

Figure 20. World Cup, 2013. 1st place - Anna Rizatdinova (Ukraine), 2nd place - Yana Kudryavtseva (Russia), 3rd place - Margarita Mamun (Russia)

CHAPTER 30

REACHING FOR THE STARS

After the World Championship, we went to the Aeon Cup in Japan. I felt very confident because I was a world champion. I forgot about tears, doubts, and uncertainty. From Japan, I brought a bronze medal for all-around events. It became clear that I was not going to finish my career. In my head, I saw a new stage, a way to the Olympic Games in Brazil, and understood that if I could keep myself at the top-3 of the World's Rhythmic Gymnastics leaders for all four years, it would be possible to go to Rio. The fourth place was not enough. It is easy to take off, but staying on the top requires tremendous effort. And, frankly speaking, I was scared.

I am a person who always sets goals. My first goal was to get into the Deriugina School and become the first number of the National Team and the first in the world. So, step by step, I entered the world of the Rhythmic Gymnastics elite. Only one most cherished dream was left, to get an Olympic medal. And this dream came true; I just needed another four years.

What does being a part of the Rhythmic Gymnastics elite mean for four years? It means never finding excuses. But we all are just human beings. Indeed, sometimes we are exhausted or unwilling to go on. We may give up in despair or be overwhelmed. Stress or lousy mood may interfere with our plans. But this is the difference between champions and average athletes; there is no excuse for a champion. They will find the motivation to work their guts out.

My most desirable goal was to get a medal in Rio. I imagined the Olympic rings before me and realized it would be completely different. If in London Olympics were gloomy and grey for me, I hoped Rio would be bright, sunny, and full of happiness and joy in my imagination. Even though I had never been there, I drew a perfect picture. I even created a photo collage called "dream-cities" and attached it to the wall in my room. Then, when it was hard to get up in the morning after exhausting training, I looked at the painting of the medal, the Olympic rings, saying "Rio."

After that, I would become so motivated that I immediately jumped out of bed. I thought, "Now you may skip a training; it's not a big deal. You can tell coaches that you feel bad and won't come today. But your rival will be brushing up on all routines at this time, and when the time for medals comes, God, who sees everything, will give a medal to that girl, not to you because she was working, but you were being lazy."

As a religious person, I was terrified of God's eyes. I believed that if I didn't work at full stretch, it could blow up in my face one day. So, I tried my best to have a clean conscience for the following four years.

A champion has no right to give up, be lazy, get sick, or make mistakes. So I set a rule: to bring at least one medal from every competition. It would be a disaster if I came home without an award.

My family, Ireesha and Nina Yeresko helped me to cope with stress. Now I could take it more manageable. Failures and disappointments happen sometimes; this is a part of the process. But then, any loss was deathlike. It was all or nothing. From time to time, a jam-packed schedule and an abandonment of life pleasures for the sake of Rhythmic Gymnastics drove me up the wall.

When girls were going to the cinema with their boyfriends, I was on my way to the gym. That is why I suffer emotional breakdowns sometimes. Although my way of thinking, on the one hand, was affecting my mental health. On the other hand, it led me to my dream.

For this reason, it is hard to say if it was a wrong decision to shut myself off the world to sacrifice everything for the sport. It worked out for me. Other girls with romantic relationships didn't take it all so close to heart. Everyone had their history.

Tough competition inside our team helped me to achieve more in sports. Alina Maksymenko, a striking gymnast of the Deriugina School, was my rival number one. Both of us got a lot of awards in 2013. Coaches admitted our progress. It has been well said, "Oaks grow among other oaks." We experienced real battles between us. We were entirely different. Alina Maksymenko was good at apparatus handling; I earned my points through skillful body movements and signature pirouettes. Even fans split into two batches: some supported Alina, and others supported me. And it was very inspiring.

Albina Deriugina had her recipe for success, "A celebrity can't be raised alone, all by herself. So it's essential to train two-three gymnasts simultaneously. Only tough competition can bring the result." In 2013, Alina brought medals as well. That year was successful for both of us. But Alina Maksymenko was more experienced; she already had two Olympics, and judges liked her. We were competing every single day in the gym and during tournaments.

Each of us was holding a dream and was reaching it step by step through thick and thin. We kept an eye on each other's achievements during competitions. We didn't have the option to fail on the carpet or to show up to the gym being down in the dumps, to develop a lazy attitude to the preparation process. We knew that young, ambitious gymnasts were right behind. And thanks to never-ending everyday battles, we made a lot of progress. The competition encourages growth.

Ireesha and Albina Deriugina supported me during the year. I was not afraid of Iryna Deriugina anymore. By the way, it was a real war in my team. Back then, I had no idea that this provoked that giant leap I made. I also realized that Albina Deriugina was fighting for me, and she was ready to go with me, so I did all right. And these thoughts comforted me.

I understood that after the World Championship, I'd be in the spotlight, and the main task was to hold out on this peak. I had all chances to get a medal in Rio. It wasn't a far-fetched dream; it could become real.

CHAPTER 31

SHARING A GOAL

Today I can assure you that if Ireesha hadn't moved to Kyiv in 2010 and started working with me in 2013, I might have missed the Olympics in Rio.

After my first Olympic Games in London, I needed more than a coach; I needed a mentor. I distanced myself from the outer world to the extent that I could not bear it anymore. I feared that any party or romantic relationship, walks in the park, cinemas, or concerts could harm my progress.

I distanced myself so much that, at some point, I felt I could lose my sanity. I had no friends; I was all alone. Only the rare calls from my parents were a bond with the outer world.

Ireesha came into my life when I had a vague idea about the future. Should I stay in Rhythmic Gymnastics? Should I not? She became my inspiration, my salvation, a grasp of fresh air. She rescued me from ordinary life and showed me a new unknown world in which she lived. Despite ten years age gap, I was always very comfortable around her. She returned from America with valuable life experience and an excellent education. She is a fascinating person who shared many things with me. As it turned out to be, there was a whole world outside of Rhythmic Gymnastics.

I was able to get distracted from my training routine, my everyday torture. It allowed me to destress and recharge. Ireesha became my friend, teacher, coach, therapist, and mother, all in one person. I found new emotions and energy to move on. I started to enjoy the training again.

I intuitively trusted Ireesha's judgment. Nobody managed to break this trust, although there were a lot of rumors around her, doubting her coaching skills, education, and knowledge of Rhythmic Gymnastics. We received a lot of criticism and threats like, "Sooner or later, the two of you will get yourselves into trouble." However, I was not scared. I had every confidence in her even though she had no formal coaching experience; she hadn't prepared any gymnasts or accompanied them to contests, especially at the Olympic Games. But, for some reason, I had a good feeling about her. I knew she would help me to get to where I wanted to be.

It's hard to explain how close we were. We were like one. We were so connected we could finish each other's sentences, text each other all night, and always have fun. We met in the right place, at the right time. Both of us were seeking our true selves. Two personalities with rich inner lives formed an inspiring alliance.

Sometimes I asked myself, "What does Ireesha gain from all of it? Why did she need it?" When she realized the extent of the potential success of working together, she became highly cooperative. She wanted to prove herself and show her mother and grandmother that she could contribute to the National Team. As a result, we won my Olympic medal. So, it means we both made the right choice by choosing each other.

We could discuss various topics, and she would invite me to concerts, exhibitions, and museums. She didn't overload me with Rhythmic Gymnastics. Instead, she revealed the world of artists, singers, dancers, and designers, a door I hadn't opened before. Before the Olympic Games, on the National Team departure day, Ireesha invited me to Madonna's concert in Kyiv. I refused to go because I feared it could overwhelm me with emotions. Now I regret it.

She helped me to grow as an athlete and a person. I used to come over to her house, and we would talk about everything, but we would work our fingers to the bone when necessary. I even got some emotional attachment to her. I couldn't train when she wasn't there in the gym anymore. Girls used to tease me, "Look, Ireesha is coming. Annie is about to start running routines finally." They were right. When I saw her, my mood looked up. I would get stamina and an inspiration to work.

Of course, Iryna Deriugina didn't like it. But there was no secret: Ireesha became the first person who didn't just listen to me but heard me; she understood me and felt what music I would fancy and what movements I needed. It was the first time I asked for advice and got the most warm and emotional response, based on my mental state. Our work together proved that inside a timid girl like me, there is a treasure box. It was closed before, but finally, Ireesha managed to find a key.

When Ireesha recalls our so-called submergence, she admits it didn't happen quickly. She said, "I saw that Annie was demanded to do something she couldn't. She lacked some particular knowledge. It was important to give her the right information to decide what she wanted and see the light at the end of the tunnel. It was necessary to fill her soul with music, culture, and communication. She needed to reveal her inner self. I saw strength, power, and energy inside of her, but she had no access to them. Yes, she became sweaty during the training and worked, but what was the outcome? No result. Annie didn't know how it felt to raise her eyes, see the world around her, see herself in that world to understand herself and learn what she could do."

"During the preparation process for London, I already felt that mission inside me. I felt like I had a chance to reveal her. Neither coaches nor judges noticed her. But she was eager to learn. I knew that after the Olympic Games, she would face difficulties. But I didn't expect her to quit. And then, when we returned to Kyiv, out of nowhere, she said it was over, and she was leaving. I thought it was mad and pretended I hadn't heard. I was not going to become her therapist. But even then, I realized that as a coach in the training process, I would only help cope with mental problems through work. I was not interested in her past, future, her dreams. I was interested in what she was at that moment. If you live connected to who you are, you can make your dream come true".

A coach is not a supervisor who controls you with a whip and tells you what you do right and wrong. You should be able to share your secrets with this person, who can provide you with advice and with whom you can cry or share everything. But, most importantly, this person would help you succeed.

There were absolutely no secrets between Ireesha and me. I trusted her completely. As soon as the coach entered the gym, I would run to hug her and be so happy she came. It was a natural feeling of happiness. Ireesha did all she could to work with me; she sacrificed much for the collective result. When her daughter was born, I saw that she often left her family and a baby to go to competitions with me. It was hard to realize and accept such a sacrifice. Nevertheless, I felt obliged to get medals, and I got them.

Our bond became so strong it was enough for her to glance at me, and I immediately understood what she wanted. A month before the Olympics, I could tell her, "Ireesha, I'm scared." I shared my secrets, fears, and feelings with her, and she helped. We had one dream for two.

Being quite ambitious, it was also crucial for Ireesha to go through this and become a winner with me, to get a wanted Olympic Games medal. That's why we achieved it. The desire to achieve results was huge. We even trained at the weekends.

She checked every step, brushed up on every movement, every turn of the head in my program. She was checking if I was moving in tune and beat. She always honestly said if something was wrong. When she noticed me being in a bad mood in the morning, she helped me start training correctly. Methods were different: sometimes music, sometimes nice words, care, and attention. All these worked well.

Naturally, sometimes we didn't get on well. Ireesha is known as a tender, soft, sentimental woman, but the most assertive person I've ever seen is hidden under this cover. I witnessed different Ireeshas. She could be angry, and she could raise her voice when it was necessary. She could forgive me for my bad mood or fatigue but never ignored unfair treatment. People's relationships were essential to her, so she had sufficient requirements.

I wasn't supposed to hide anything from my coach. I am not the easiest person to deal with. Sometimes I self-isolate. For instance, when Ireesha worked with other girls, I could become jealous or disapprove of her when she criticized me. If Ireesha didn't show up, I resented it. But with her, I was learning how to manage my emotions.

We have gone through a lot and carried out a revolution. Before, there were only two coaches in the Deriugina School, Albina Deriugina and Iryna Deriugina. It was unacceptable for a coach to train only one or two gymnasts. But we did it. Ireesha was known as a choreographer rather than as a coach.

We agreed that Ireesha would accompany me to the contests. Before the start, I always needed her inner tranquility, not emotional swings. Ireesha resembles her grandmother Albina Deriugina a lot: they both are discreet and persistent. You would never tell, even if they shake like a leaf inside because of fear. Some were stunned by hot-headed Iryna Deriugina, but I needed a more laid-back approach, and Ireesha Deriugina could give me that.

At the 2013 World Championship, Albina Deriugina accompanied me. Ireesha was staying behind the curtains. Few people noticed her even though she was the one who had been preparing me. Before the Olympic Games, there were doubts about whether Ireesha could present me in such a big contest. What if she got lost in a moment of great importance? But I was firm, "If I go to Rio, I will be accompanied only by Ireesha and no one else." Others accepted it, and we succeeded.

Still, her way of coaching was indeed revolutionary. In the beginning, many people didn't understand her. Her approach to coaching is unusual. She likes checking everything slowly, explaining, and brushing up. Not every gymnast would like it, but it worked perfectly for me. Sometimes I received questions like, "How can you be serious about her? She is not a coach, is she?" The debates were long, but the result speaks for itself.

Day by day, we were growing closer. Sometimes I felt like we were sisters, later like she was my mother. My feelings for her were so warm that I wished her to adopt me. Being friends is not enough; good energy is crucial. Lovers share a magical bond of affection. I can say the same about friendship: whether you feel each other or not. We felt each other. We were friends.

When a child is told for years, "You are grey, not emotional enough, your legs are too short, instep is wrong, you lack stretching," the child starts believing in it. Then, suddenly, another person says, "You are a diamond in a raw. You are unique."

When your eyes open, you realize that you are also gifted. With such a realization, people can move mountains. It is so important when someone believes in you. A gymnast is not a robot; she is alive. Albina Deriugina really believed in me, and that's why we got on well. I wanted to achieve more with her.

I devoted my performance at the 2014 Europe Championship to Ireesha entirely. She was pregnant then, and I appreciated her accompanying me everywhere. But, I worried that stress could affect her pregnancy somehow. So, I was praying to get a medal.

In three years, in 2015, Ireesha was finally recognized as my coach. It brought me joy. I was very happy for her. I was very grateful to God for sending me Ireesha while standing on the edge of a precipice.

CHAPTER 32

WAR

For Ukraine and all Ukrainians, 2014 was scary and unexpected. Our training was held in the October Palace. Euromaidan was happening a few blocks away from us. The number of tents and bonfires was growing in front of our eyes. People were wearing balaclavas, and a special police force, Berkut, was reaching the square from the other side to stop riots. Yet, time passed, and in a few weeks, the demonstrators set their tents at the October Palace territory.

They set up a mobile kitchen trailer in the parking lot near the October Palace and organized a dining area. From the very first days, we witnessed how the camp town grew and how more people arrived. Honestly, it was a scary scene. I remember we came to the gym and found broken doors, dirty Olympic carpets that once were snow white, and apparatus lying all over the gym. Somebody had broken the door, and the crowd had been seeking something. We were frightened. We didn't feel safe because different people gathered together, not only those fighting for civil rights but also criminals.

It was extremely tough for Ukraine: revolution and then war. As a matter of fact, athletes were the ones who probably felt the consequences more than others. I remember when during the training, Iryna Deriugina received a call from the Ministry of Sports; she was encouraged to cancel all the events and to send gymnasts home. Martial law was declared. No one knew what to expect: panic was spreading. It was a shock and a disaster for us.

Usually, the beginning of the year, February, is a crucial period for athletes, the Olympic Games preparation process. So, what did it mean not to attend the gym? My rivals would enhance their skills, but I would stay home and do nothing.

The coaches decided to move the team to Simferopol and continue to train us. Why did we choose this city exactly? There is an excellent Olympic gym in Simferopol, even better than in Kyiv. At that time, it was calm and peaceful there. So, with my Mom in the lead, girls started to train individual programs in Crimea.

We spent three weeks there until the situation in Kyiv improved, then we returned to the capital. In March, I went to Budapest to participate in a competition. Russia annexed the Crimean Peninsula from Ukraine during the World Championship in Hungary. The fate of the Crimeans was at stake. I worried, failed my performance, and took second place, although my main rivals, Russian athletes, didn't participate. My heart was with Crimea, with my parents. I was begging God not to allow war to start there. Crimea is part of Ukraine, and it will always be so.

The first part of 2014 I marked with black color: with fear, dark balaclavas, fire, intense smoke, explosions, the loss of home, and people's deaths, which is more frightening. Yet, right in this challenging time, every Ukrainian athlete transformed into a true patriot. We were obsessed with raising our national flag in every competition to prove that we, as a nation, didn't give up and continued to fight.

In 2014 we created a beautiful ribbon routine, Carmen. Spectators always loved it. I also adored this routine. It was so outstanding that I performed it for two years. The process of creating it was also unique. Everyone knows that Iryna Deriugina's favorite topic is Carmen. As Maya Plisetskaya is associated with it in ballet, Iryna Deriugina in Rhythmic Gymnastics is associated with a Spanish dance pasodoble full of gypsy passion and a red rose in her hair. She was enjoying my Carmen.

We realized that we had to make my Carmen perfect. In the beginning, we worked on the technical part. Then we started precisely working on dance step combinations. Iryna Deriugina did her best! She was absolutely in charge, and she did well. We used an unusual source for help - Maya Plisetskaya herself. We learned dance steps from the video recorded by the ballerina step by step and, of course, added our movements. Iryna Deriugina analyzed, thought it through, and matched it all together. As a result, we got a powerful routine.

In June 2014 European Championship was held in Baku, Azerbaijan. It turned out to be quite a challenge for me. We were competing for one medal in all-around routines. I wouldn't say I liked a contest with no finals. I love finals. It allows an athlete to speed up: if you fail in one routine, you still have a chance to succeed in the next one.

In finals, gymnasts have four opportunities to fight for a medal. But in Baku, we worked day and night for one trophy only. I hope we'll see finals in the Olympic program sometime—everyone involved in Rhythmic Gymnastics dreams about it.

Mentally it was tough to be completely ready to perform only once. You had to concentrate on having only one day, one attempt. There was no tomorrow, only today. Usually, after all-around events, I felt mentally drained.

In Baku, I started with a ribbon routine, Carmen. Unfortunately, I could have performed better. I was agitated and even cried behind the curtains. I could forget about winning medals. But then I did a hoop, ball, and club routine well. One of the biggest mistakes of many gymnasts is that they think it's over if they fail the first routine. Many athletes give up if they don't see a chance to get a medal.

It happened to me many times. But experience has proven that sometimes things can be very unpredictable. It happens that the most robust athletes make mistakes in the Olympic Games. Nerves, stress, and a new climate: can all affect an athlete's performance. And the one who, after a failure, will concentrate on the following three routines will win. It is vital not to give up!

Having performed a ribbon routine, I accepted defeat. However, it took a long time for me to return to my senses. Although in this contest, Ireesha accompanied me, she was pregnant at the time, so we didn't mean to make her nervous. But I had a nervous breakdown. Ireesha didn't even know how to calm me down. Then she got a brilliant idea, "Now pray to the Holy Father for protection!"

It made me feel much better, and I performed the subsequent three routines, feeling the Divine would help. However, waiting for my score was very tough. My medal was at stake. I sat in front of the screen, praying to keep third place. It would have been a disaster if I had gotten a wooden award. I was so nervous that I was talking to myself, repeating, "Please, not the fourth place, not the fourth."

An Israeli gymnast Neta Rivkin performed after me. The difference between our scores was so slight. At this moment, Liubov Charkashyna, an all-around bronze medalist of the Olympic Games in London and the president of the FIG Athletes' Commission, who was sitting the closest to the screen and was watching the last part of the competition, turned around and said, "That's it. You are the third!".

Figure 21. Italy, Pesaro.

I asked her, "Are you sure?" One of the girls commented, "No, wait, you are the fourth." So then, the judges needed to decide whether I take third or fourth place. Finally, I became the third. I cried and thanked Lord for supporting me.

In September, we went to the World Championship in Izmir. I was anxious. Albina Deriugina was the one who accompanied me in the competition; Ireesha didn't go. It was so hard for me; I had just started to feel that strong bond between us. But she had already told me she was expecting a baby and couldn't come to Hungary. I knew we had to separate for some time, and this thought burdened me. Everything went so well only when she was near. Her absence traumatized me.

However, we always kept in touch; I told her about my training, feelings, and performances. I found the vibe of the competition calming. The sports complex looked cozy and nicely designed in purple colors. Being there felt like warm wind covering my body, cheering me a little.

The night before the contest, I dedicated some time to myself, especially my mental health. For me, the day before a significant competition is always stressful. I experienced constant anxiety and many doubts like "What if I failed? What if something goes wrong? What should I do then?"

In Izmir, I went to the sea and spent some time on the shore listening to the waves, talking to God, and thinking about a positive outcome, and it helped me to loosen up. Then, at last, I felt confident and strong.

The first competition day was hard; there were hoop and ball finals. Even though the hoop was one of my best routines, I ended up without medals. It discouraged me greatly. I realized that I had only three attempts left. The following day was more successful. I performed tremendously and won awards: a bronze for clubs and ribbon routines, a bronze for all-around events, and a bronze for team events.

So, all my worries were useless. But this is how I am. I used to dig an emotional hole for myself; perhaps it comes from my Zodiac sign, Cancer. Such people are very gentle and sensitive and care deeply about everything; they overthink. But sometimes, turning on the "I don't care" sassy attitude is essential.

Unfortunately, it is atypical for me. Before the start, thoughts are always raging in my head; my whole life flashes before my eyes. So an athlete must separate worries from them to merge into one with an apparatus. For me, this is a success already! I used to be mentally squeezed before the start because I had been fighting against myself.

CHAPTER 33

SUCCESSFUL OVERNIGHT

The year 2015 wasn't without surprises. An athlete could qualify for an Olympic license that year, so I worked even harder than usual. The 2015 European Games, an international multi-sport event for athletes representing the National Olympic Committees, were first held in Baku in June. It became a crucial contest for me. It is like a mock version of the Olympics; it also takes place every four years, and athletes live in the Olympic Village.

We concentrated solely on training. However, I felt like I was in some haze. A scary thought appeared: "It will be like the Olympic Games. What if I have already burned out? It happens to athletes." In Baku, the fear covered me up. Ireesha wasn't there; her daughter Jacqueline was just born so she couldn't come.

Albina Deriugina also was absent, so Iryna Deriugina accompanied me. The team shared a common goal; we had to sacrifice our personal wishes for the collective good. But, for some reason, I was suspicious and expected some trouble initially. I was right.

My first performance was with a hoop. I made a mistake by doing a pirouette while catching the apparatus. I was lost; it was a disaster. Then, I started a ball routine, already upset. So, no surprise, I ended up with only two medals in the European Games: a silver medal for clubs and a silver one for a ball. Any other gymnast would be happy, but not me. I was so mentally exhausted that I couldn't bear it anymore. I understand now that my behavior was inappropriate. It could have been much more relaxed and positive.

I invented imaginary difficulties myself. When I lost an apparatus once, I panicked. I couldn't accept it or pretend nothing had happened. In sports, people learn from mistakes. Being grateful for every failure is vital because it can teach you a lesson I understood only in 2016. But, unfortunately, it was already too late.

Believe it or not, having analyzed all situations, I noticed that after something terrible happened to me, like a failed performance or an emotional breakdown, I made a significant and fundamental breakthrough.

I visited the Korean city Gwangju in July to participate in the Universiade. Albina Deriugina accompanied me, so I felt calm. A competition between a Korean gymnast and me was about to start. Until 2015 I understood who my main rivals were: two Russians, Margarita Mamun and Yana Kudryavtseva, a Belarusian gymnast Melitina Staniouta and a Korean athlete Son Yeon-jae. To beat a Korean on her territory was challenging, but I tried. I got a gold medal for clubs, a silver for a ball routine, a silver for all-around, and a bronze for a ribbon. However, my complex personality didn't allow me to enjoy my medals because Son Yeon-jae exceeded me in three events.

On the bright side, I found an extraordinary present when I returned to Kyiv. The mural depicted Ukrainian gymnast Anna Rizatdinova on the corner of Striletska and Stritenska streets near Zoloti Vorota, the Golden Gate of Kyiv. It was Fintan Magee's, an Australian street artist's creation. His murals are famous throughout Australia, the UK, Germany, Ireland, Colombia, Russia, etc. It was a pleasant surprise that made me happy.

I want to mention one more World championship in Stuttgart. It was the last competition before the Olympic Games. My anxiety level was high, and I needed to get into top-3 in all-around events. Ireesha came with me. She was traveling with her husband and a little daughter Jackie. I knew they were doing it for me, which made me feel even more responsible for the outcome. I had to win those medals, whatever it took.

We started with finals. I always needed to get a medal after the first performance. Then it was mentally much easier to continue, "No matter what happens next, I have at least one medal to bring home." This time it was exactly like this. I won a medal for a hoop routine on the first day, and the fear of failure faded away. Then I got two more awards for clubs and a ribbon.

I was very optimistic about all-around events because, before the contest, I had developed a conscientious attitude to the training process. I had got all routines down to a fine art. I started with clubs. According to the grades, clubs were my best. Everything was going well. I had to do a complicated and risky element at the end of the routine. Right before the last beat of the music, I swung a leg with force, and clubs flew away beyond the carpet.

The audience sighed. So did I. I finished the routine without apparatus. It hadn't happened to me for many years. Music was off; I went behind the stage, picked up my clubs, and waved them to the audience. They tried to cheer for me, applauding, but I felt a growing avalanche of shame. It's impossible to describe what it's like to disappoint so many people. It hurt so much, and there was nothing I could do to change it.

I realized I let down people, my country, and the coaches and blamed myself for it. This accident seemed strange, sudden, and unexpected; I practiced the final difficult element to a dot and could do it with my eyes closed. No matter how I tried to analyze that unfortunate accident, I couldn't find the answer. It was tough to accept because I had nailed that routine many times before and won trophies.

Unfortunately, it was the first performance out of four. After such a failure, forcing yourself to perform other routines is almost impossible. It can be hard to find reasons to fight. I went backstage, threw my clubs away, and burst into tears. Ireesha tried to calm me down. But there were no words that could help. Then Ireesha and I agreed that I would no longer compete for medals that day. However, I still could win; other girls also made mistakes. But we set a different goal: I had to fight for an Olympic license because I was about to lose it.

I started the following routine, being in 15th place. It was crucial to perform the second program excellently to get enough points. I managed to do it, although I performed with tear-stained eyes doing everything without emotions. Hence, I became the fifth and got my license. Later I understood that I could have become the third if I had performed at least with a smile. It was too evident to the judges that I was devastated after the first failure.

CHAPTER 34

NO GYM FOR ME

After returning home, it was hard to forget about the failure. It wasn't an accident, and it was probably a bad sign. Perhaps, I had to go through it before the Olympic Games to feel I could not relax. I recently won many medals, which played a cruel joke on me.

Since 2014 I never got back home empty-handed. I have already secured my place in the top 3 of the world's Rhythmic Gymnastics. I needed badly to keep up, as the most substantial world gymnasts were at my heels. Only a hundred points separated us. So, I had to think of something and fast. Soon I had three contests per month at the time, all of which were important.

Before the World Championship in September, I never rested for the whole summer, working my fingers to the bone. There was simply no time. The Club Championship in Japan was coming, and we needed a new program afterward. We had the same schedule for years. Such a crazy lifestyle, alongside physical and emotional overload, often causes emotional breakdowns.

One of the breakdowns happened to me in 2015 before the European Championship in Minsk. What could go wrong? But a week before the contest, one fine day, I woke up and felt I didn't want to go to the gym. I couldn't help it.

My Mom was in Kyiv at the moment. I remember she was pulling me out of bed. I cried because I had no energy to get up and go to the gym. Can you imagine such emotional swings? One day it was impossible to get me out of the gym; the next day, Mom tried to send me there hopelessly.

153

She finally managed to drive me to the training somehow. But in the gym, it got worse: I had to take apparatus in my hands, and I couldn't. I remember putting a club on a shoulder, then the music turned on, but I stopped and started crying because I couldn't continue.

I didn't want to move; I felt nauseous, knowing I reached my limit. You may ask, "What about your motivation?" Yes, I had a goal, but at the moment, I had forgotten everything: my dreams and plans. I just felt sick of the gym, the surrounding, and everything happening around me. I craved some rest; I wanted to escape and do something for a change. Sometimes a change of scenery helps to cope with stress. But in my case, no one would approve days off and one week left before the European Championship.

Everyone around me used various methods to help, but nothing helped. I had no energy to continue, and no argument could change my mind. I was drowning more profoundly in my neverending loop of thoughts.

My dearest people know that I am a religious person. Knowing that a conversation with God isn't empty words for me, they decided that holy places might help. The coaches devised an idea to take me to the Kyiv Pechersk Lavra. I was wandering around Lavra for some time, having reached the Far Caves; after praying next to the relics of the Pechersk saints, the miracle happened: I suddenly felt better.

Then I went to the gym again. Everyone wondered, "Did it work? Is she doing better?" Slowly I took the apparatus and started the exercise. But, sure thing, God has eyes, so I wasn't looking forward to a miracle in the European Championship. I made a couple of severe mistakes during my performances. Though we still won a medal in group events and finals for four routines, I earned only one silver medal. Thank God for that. The result reflected my preparation.

Looking back, I get chills. How many ups and downs I went through? How many times have I wanted to give up and leave?

There are no coincidences in sports! Even unforeseen and weird failures happen on purpose. They make us mentally and physically stronger. The struggle is a part of spiritual growth. I have always believed that one wins a fight, not in the moment of competition but long before it. So every time you cheat in the gym, don't work at full stretch; at the moment of utmost importance, it will reveal itself. But, as it is said in Ukraine, "If you lose, at least learn the lesson."

CHAPTER 35

CHANCES OF GOING TO RIO

In November 2015, we flew to Brazil. A tournament was held between Brazil and Ukraine in the state's capital of Espirito Santo, Vitoria. This trip was vital before the Olympic Games because it could help us understand how our bodies would react to a new climate. We needed to check how we would feel and how our bodies would take humidity and heat. We also had to check how the apparatus would adjust, especially the balls and ribbons.

It was my first time in Brazil, and I was incredibly impressed. It was something new, bright, exotic, and never-seen-before. We felt the Brazilian vibe, culture, customs, and people.

The National Brazilian Team group events coach conducted a three-hour-long lesson on Brazilian samba for us. A beautiful Brazilian woman was demonstrating the critical movements of this dance. At first, it seemed pretty straightforward, but later we felt how difficult it is to move hips at a frantic pace. It would help if you were born and raised in this sunny country to dance like her. But we learned some samba basics, which later the team added to its group events.

Samba lessons came in handy during the creation of the Olympic program. We were lucky enough to see with our own eyes that Brazilians are on fire; rhythm is in their blood, and emotions live in their hearts. So precisely after this trip, we came up with an idea to use the rhythm of Brazilian drums and create a program with elements of hot samba.

I tried to do my best in Vitoria, expressed myself in the best light, enjoyed my performances, and was happy to perform in such a prestigious competition. My long, arduous journey was already behind me, while faith in myself and victory awaited. I pursued this goal for many years through failures, pain, non-recognition, and disfavor of coaches and judges. Now I am the first number in the country.

I didn't even allow myself to think that one day Iryna Deriugina would be helping me, and we would find common ground and get on well. The competition had just finished, and it was all about pleasure. I have checked how the apparatus reacts to humidity and understood that it's pretty hard to work with ribbon. It would turn wet, heavy, and tangling.

Having considered this, later, I was making a ribbon wet at home on purpose. In fact, since the beginning of 2016, all gymnasts in our team had to work with two ribbons. When you work with two and after you take one of the ribbons away, the routine becomes more apparent.

I asked Iryna Deriugina to get us air conditioners installed. It was vital to get used to them. We realized it was boiling in Brazil in summer when air conditioners were on in Rio, which is terrible for ribbons. I had to be ready because airflow could blow the apparatus. Iryna Deriugina did what I asked. We had an opportunity to go through all the hidden pitfalls beforehand. Air conditioners were on while we were working with the apparatus.

I felt I was on the final straight; the Olympic Games fluttered forward and charged me extra energy. The foretaste of the most critical contest was warming my feelings up. Time seemed to shrink, and the less time I had, the scarier it was. But I knew I was ready and consciously moving toward it.

The training was no longer disappointing or tiring. The great motivation was leading me forward, and in my mind, I was already in Rio. Going to bed, I begged God for only one thing: "Please, help me! I am ready to overcome difficulties, go through everything you've prepared for me, help me do everything well in Rio, and get a medal." As soon as I opened my eyes in the morning, I had only one thought, "I will win a medal in Rio!"

My desire was so strong that I literally lived for it. I remember we had a tour organized in Rio-de-Janeiro; we went to the top of Corcovado mountain to the statue of Jesus Christ. People were looking at the city from above, taking pictures, and laughing, but I begged God for an Olympic medal.

Later, in 2016, when we went to the European Championship in Israel, I went to Jerusalem to see the Wailing Wall. Afterward, I left a note asking to become a medalist at the Olympic Games.

CHAPTER 36

THE OLYMPIC PROGRAM

The last month of 2015 was also stressful because we started to create a new program. We all realized that the coming year was the Olympics, and the program had to be victorious. Coaches and gymnasts both worked hard. Every year this process was becoming more and more complicated.

Iryna Deriugina and Ireesha suggested the song I Put a Spell On You by Annie Lennox for my ball routine. I dug in my heels on it. Shortly before this, the movie Fifty Shades of Grey was released, using the song as a theme. I subconsciously associated the music with the film, which was distracting me. We had a little argument; I wanted a different piece and suggested other options. But the coaches stood firm, only this music!

Iryna Deriugina said, "I have gone through eight Olympic cycles. What are you trying to prove to me?" I had no choice but to agree and work. Ireesha and I knew very well that everything should be new and unique. Dance step combinations had to be modern and unconventional. Then we decided to invite Oleg Zhezhel from the Ukrainian dance team Kazaky for help; he had already worked with us before.

Iryna Deriugina was okay with the idea. For the first time, I danced with Kazaky in 2013 at the gala concert of the World Championship in Kyiv. In 2014 Oleg often came over to the gym. He taught gymnasts to express emotions via movements more exquisitely, showing some helpful dance combinations. His lessons changed with energy. It was Ireesha's wise decision to invite him. We all needed some inspiration, which Oleg provided.

His choreography lessons were a good kick for our team's further development. Together, we prepared various elements of dance steps and movements. Moreover, he helped me to find a proper style. After his appearance in the gym, I started to like, just a while ago, the repulsive song of Annie Lennox and fashion.

I rebelled against it for some more time, but I gave in when we found the proper dance steps and combined all the elements into a beautiful choreography. But, frankly speaking, my creative pursuit made everyone around crazy. The routine was luminous and extraordinary. Later it became for me the most favorite one of all my routines.

Figure 22. My Olympic performance with ribbon in Rio, 2016.

Working with a ribbon was also a pleasure. Although Oleg modified some of the Samba movements, we brought from Brazil, trying to make my image more dazzling. I fancied his ideas and joined the creation process with great pleasure.

We chose a familiar Spanish style for my hoop routine. Everyone liked the idea, but we still were searching for good music. Iryna Deriugina suggested Pasodoble, a Spanish dance inspired by a bullfight. The music was so inspiring that I got a second breath and immediately realized: that's what we were looking for!

However, with clubs, it was challenging. We couldn't agree on something for a long time. At first, we chose a Spanish classical melody and created a routine, I performed it for a month, but the music didn't catch the ear of the listener and didn't bring out emotions. And in spring, before the World Cup in Brazil, we decided to change it completely. Ireesha and I tried to explain to Iryna Deriugina that we had to choose something catchier.

Ireesha knew I had adored Michael Jackson since childhood and had already created some routines for his music. This time we went for They Do Not Care About Us. It is very dynamic. The important thing was that the music video for this song had been shot in Brazil, in Rio, and the song's central idea was a hot topic in the country that had been developing fast but remained poor.

"The song is about the pain of prejudice and hate and is a way to draw attention to social and political problems. It is the voice of the accused and the attacked", said the singer. This time we got no objections. Everyone understood immediately that this was what we needed. Although changing a routine in the middle of the season is risky, we managed to accomplish this.

CHAPTER 37

WHAT IF RIZATDINOVA BURNS OUT?

At the end of 2015, after returning home from Brazil, I realized that the most important event of my life was about to begin. A strange feeling of fear covered me: I was afraid to run out of time, and I worried that my rivals would prepare themselves better and get higher in the competition rate than me.

I was obsessed with these ideas and pushed myself to work harder. There were a lot of rumors about my program; they said it was too easy to make mistakes. So, during the Olympic year, our primary goal was to make it more complicated. But, honestly, mastering new elements at 23 is far more complex than at 17.

I decided not to wait until fear possessed me and went to the sports store to buy a cold-weather tracksuit, some running gear, fitness compression clothes for the gym (to warm up muscles faster), and 1,5lb (700g) weight cuffs, as 0,6lb (300g) wasn't enough for me.

In December, the weather was below-freezing outside in Kyiv, but I didn't care. Instead, I decided to go running in the mornings. The first training began at 9 in the morning; at 7:30, I had to be at the stadium.

Ten circles in freezing weather. It was challenging; frosty air irritated my skin, but I kept running. Then I would drop into the car and go to the gym. Nobody could understand why my face was all red after I entered the room.

But my body told me it wasn't for nothing, and a morning run worked. I praised myself for being diligent and goal-oriented. My legs became more flexible, and my routine became more dynamic. That was necessary for a ribbon samba performance. After an everyday run, my legs flew, and I built even more stamina. After two weeks, I could do a full repetition circle, despite the pace being crazy.

I was running out of time, but I had to do more than others. During the Olympic year, I worked until I dropped out. The coaches were delighted with my excellent shape. Every January, we used to go to Los Angeles for the International tournament. Everyone adored this contest: the beginning of the season in the United States, a new program trial. I needed to win as I had said: if I won here, the following year would be very successful.

We were competing with the Belarusian team. I craved to exceed one of my main rivals, Melitina Staniouta. And I did it; I won in all-around events. The victory brought me confidence.

Iryna Deriugina later told me that the judges asked her, "Don't you worry that Rizatdinova burns out?" Typically, athletes tend to it. It's vital to be in your best physical condition exactly before the Olympic Games, not earlier, not later. That is why every champion has a team of professionals who skillfully lead them to their best shape up to the particular date. But I started the year so actively that many thought I would only keep that pace briefly. However, my desire and aspiration to win were increasing every month.

After the USA, we went to Estonia to participate in the International competition Miss Valentine, where I collected all the awards. Still, the point was that my main rivals didn't participate in that contest.

In the World Cup in Finland, I got third place in all-around events, the first for hoop and ribbon finals, the second for the final with clubs, and the third for the ball.

Although only some things were proceeding smoothly, as I would wish, inner pressure was growing, and sometimes I would lose my temper. For example, there was an argument between Iryna Deriugina and me at the airport Boryspil at the beginning of March. We went to Milan to get to Desio to participate in the competition between Italy and Ukraine. Iryna Deriugina commented on my clothes; she underlined that I wasn't wearing a jacket from our sponsoring brand. I took it personally like an undeserved reason for an argument.

We were already at the departure lounge 15 minutes before boarding. Viktoria Mazur, the second number on our team, was sitting next to me, and I told her that I was leaving; she smiled and added, "Where are you going?" I picked up my suitcase and went to the exit. Viktoria called after me, "You cannot be serious!" I replied, "Oh, yes! I can!" and speeded up.

Border guards at the passport control desk were shocked, "Excuse me, where are you going?" I replied that I wouldn't fly. They glanced at me suspiciously and asked, "Why?" I made up a story, "Something has come up at home; I have to go back."

They showed me the way through the staff exit, and I also worked out an issue with my baggage; it was already off the flight. After some time, coaches realized that one gymnast was missing. After that, everyone started calling me, but I canceled all their calls. I rode in the taxi, as far as possible from the conflict. It was my kind of protest.

I have never understood why someone should moralize a diligent, dedicated adult who does their best to achieve results. It is okay to lecture kids. When we were younger, we used to have guidance. But when an athlete has already achieved a lot and is not a teenager, it's better to refrain from lecturing them. Then, they can fight back, as happened in my case. If something was wrong, I was ready to leave.

Mom called from Crimea. Ireesha and Nina, who stayed in Kyiv, kept calling me, too. Finally, three of them calmed me down and persuaded me not to be at odds with the National Team's head coach. The following day I arrived at the contest. We talked with Iryna Deriugina; I apologized for my behavior and explained why I behaved that way. We agreed that it wasn't necessary if we liked each other; we had a common goal and were moving towards it. After this conversation, we calmed down and got on well until the Olympics.

In 2016 everything had been going on successfully before we went to Thiais, France, to participate in the Grand Prix series competition. Something strange happened to me there. Being in great shape, I failed. I performed well at a rehearsal, realizing that experts were paying particular attention to judges and that I was already making decisions on the top 3 of the world Rhythmic Gymnastics leaders. Unfortunately, I had exhausted myself before the contest so much that I had no power to fight. It was my mistake; an elite athlete has to be able to manage their energy.

Negative psychological factors also took their toll: elite gymnasts were warming up on the same carpet. This atmosphere put a lot of pressure: the presence of a large delegation from Russia and other countries.

I remember Iryna Deriugina told me, "Come on! Please show them your persistence during the rehearsal, and win! Let's go!" At that moment, those words discouraged me. I lost all contact with reality, started crying, and refused to perform. Ireesha and the coach of the Ukrainian National Team, Maryna Kardash, who had been supporting me for four years, tried to help me.

I remember Maryna came to the changing room and began to talk me into performing, "Annie, dress up, please. It's time to go to the stage". But, when I withdraw into myself, it is just impossible to get me back to normal. I was staying behind the curtains doing nothing. I went to the carpet having a tear-stained face and made mistakes.

I ended up fourth all-around, which was a total failure. I also got a bronze medal for a club's routine and a bronze one for a ribbon. But whatever happens, happens for the best. This competition pushed me to reconsider my behavior. I couldn't help thinking I had distanced myself from Ireesha in a difficult moment.

So, I had only one option: to fight my inner demons and keep my ego and ambitions in check. I told myself, "If you continue like this, you won't achieve your goal." So, after that contest, I plunged into the process so no one could stop me.

I became the third in all-around events in the World Cup in Pesaro, Italy. It was an unconditional success as I competed with the world's strongest gymnasts. Moreover, I earned two gold medals for a ball routine and a ribbon one. In addition, the Ukrainian national anthem sounded twice; we helped our flag to rise. It was so inspiring.

After that, I went to the international tournament in Corbeil-Essonnes, France, which was my triumph. I won in all stages, all-around, and finals. I brought home five gold medals. Back home in Kyiv, people called me a national heroine. People's reaction to the word "gold" is unconditional. Newspapers and magazines wrote articles about me, and TV channels and radio representatives interviewed me. I even received congratulations from the president at the time, Perto Poroshenko.

The Word Cup in Sofia was held in May, where I went without Ireesha again, with Iryna Deriugina. I felt like I was away from a mother, like a child. But I was absolutely ready for it. I performed all-around routines and finals well, so the second place overall was mine.

Before the start, Iryna Deriugina, being hot-tempered, began to push me. She was highly emotional, rushing me. Some athletes would love it, but not me. Such an approach is taboo before my performance. I need a calm, harmonious condition. But the coach made me tense; I started to work myself into a panic state and got frightened.

I came to the coach, took her hand, and said, "Please, I beg you, just calm down. I am ready. I'm going to do everything properly." It was the first time when a gymnast was comforting her coach. And the miracle happened, Iryna Deriugina had heard me; she cooled off, helped, and made corrections without excessive emotions.

When I finished all performances, I was on the verge of getting into trouble. I won second place, but the competition continued. Some of the gymnasts were still competing. Being delighted, I, wearing a tracksuit, went to the shopping mall with other girls to drink coffee and hang out. Unfortunately, the cellular network didn't work there. When I felt it was time to go, I saw dozens of text messages after we went outside, "Annie, where are you? Are you mad? Come back right now!"

We took a taxi and rushed back. Competition organizers announced an award ceremony on the same day, but we have not heard anything. Then, finally, the coaches were told, "If your gymnast doesn't show up to the award ceremony, she will be charged a penalty and stripped a medal for being late to the award ceremony." We panicked. Thank God I was jammed into a leotard and sent to the stage just in time.

In June, the annual European Championship in Israel became the season's main event before the Olympic Games. We had a week to prepare for it. No one was worried except me. "Why am I not asked to do 7-5-4-2? If I didn't do it, something unpredictable would happen." So I told Ireesha that I was going to do 7-5-4-2.

She was surprised, "Why? You do everything great. It's enough to do 4-3 repetitions for you and rest.". But I insisted. And it made a difference. A tough mental battle awaited us in Israel: that's where an Olympic podium would form. Coaches and gymnasts were anxious. I had no right to fail. Moreover, there were no finals, only one medal for all-around events.

As usual, I went out in the evening, prayed, and begged God to help. Eventually, it was good for me, but I remember that anxiety before the performance. I didn't allow myself to relax for a single moment. The competition itself and a warm-up session went on for five hours. All that time, I was agitated and concentrated. I couldn't allow myself any emotions. Finally, after finishing the last routine, I eased up, smiled, and even shed a tear because I felt happy to have accomplished everything.

I was satisfied with my performance. I needed to manage my emotions and set myself up for one performance with four routines. I did it. However, a headache because of many thoughts was more severe than the ache in the body after training.

I performed here even better than in the Olympic Games; I was more unfettered. The audience helped a lot. I earned a bronze medal in all-around events and was happy to see the National flag of Ukraine rising. When the anthem played, I wished, "God, please, let the same happen in Rio. Let the Ukrainian flag rise again, among the top 3 in the Olympics."

The year 2016 was successful for me. The program was ready, and I was in my best shape before the Olympics. Then, in the World Championship in Guadalajara, I got 19 points for the first time in my career. I still needed to get more. When you are so lucky, it is overwhelming. I was even waiting for some failure to happen. Just not in the Olympic Games, please.

Our life consists of ups and downs, like a sports career. It's impossible always to be the best. People are not robots. Even athletes. Additionally, I had that fear of failing to work on something adequately enough. So sometimes, I would come to the gym on Sunday, play different songs, and try to see how ready I was. I did repetitions of routines.

I found it calming. I did it long before 2016. My therapy was coming to the gym when it was empty and turning on inspiring music.

CHAPTER 38

COMPETING WITH MYSELF

The Olympic year is usually emotionally draining. Everyone is stressed: coaches, judges, and gymnasts. However, day X was coming, and everyone was doing their best. For me, everything was going well. I brought medals from all competitions.

Having returned from Israel, all realized it was just two months before the Olympic Games. Tension was running high. It was impossible to anticipate the prize winners; if one gymnast failed, another immediately replaced her. There were only three places on the podium. Consistency might be my strong side, my key to success.

In 2016 I scaled such heights in Rhythmic Gymnastics sport that Iryna Deriugina invited me to her office at the beginning of the season. We chose the dates for upcoming tournaments together. It was the highest point of trust between a coach and a gymnast. Then, just one month before the Olympic Games, we went to Berlin to participate in the International competition, which had yet to correspond to our schedule. I wanted to avoid coming. There were more other tournaments than enough.

I planned to stay home and prepare for the Olympic Games is a slow pace, but coaches insisted on going to Germany. I started with a ball routine and doing the most accessible element that any gymnast can do, holding a ball on the back for the ring turn; my ball flew away beyond the carpet. Imagine how I felt: one month before Rio, my whole year had been excellent, and in the end, in a contest of minor importance, I derailed all my confidence and consistency in one fell swoop!

I was desperate. I blamed everyone around. What if we had come here, we didn't have to do it, I would have been preparing for Rio being in a good mood, but now I have to cheer myself up somehow. I was fourth all-around, winning a gold medal and a silver one in the finals. But yet, I was in an awful mood.

I was highly anxious and was tying myself up in knots. Every day I would fight with myself. Not to push me over the edge and not to mess up the preparation process, I required some rest. I asked coaches to let me go for three days to hit the road, change the scenery, and meet other people. Iryna Deriugina was firmly against it.

Usually, the Deriuginas consider that rest negatively influences gymnasts, so they lose the pace, and rivals exceed them. We were rarely allowed to have at least week trips, whereas, in other countries, it is common practice to give athletes a chance to travel, sunbathe under the sun, recharge, and get back and start training with new energy. Here I felt how badly I needed some rest, to renew at least a little bit to continue. Ireesha and I began to think over this, but at the same time, I worried whether these three days might do me good.

After lengthy arguments between Ireesha and Iryna Deriugina, we won. I was allowed to go for three days, which I spent with my friends, the first number of the Hungarian National team, Dóra Vass and Nina Yeresko. We flew to Budapest, where we stayed in Dóra's family house.

The weekend was fantastic: we visited the well-known Szechenyi Baths, where I got refreshments and recreation, and we walked a lot—this leisure time worked well for me. I must say that Nina has rescued me from mental breakdowns many times. Thanks to the moments when she gave her helping hand, we became very close, like sisters.

The Olympic preparation process was ruthless. I was working with two ribbons all the time. I would go outside to try it on the wind; I was getting used to an air conditioner, and I would make a ribbon wet to make it heavier. I had to be ready to cope with any difficulties and not allow any conditions or consequences to interfere

170

with my performance. I voluntarily wore 1,7lb (700g) weight cuffs and did repetitions of routines with them.

I was the only one following the well-known plan of Albina Deriugina, 7-5-4-2. I asked to create a separate schedule for enough space on the carpet during training. Unfortunately, I was the only one representing Ukraine in the individual Rhythmic Gymnastics program. And that made me sad because it would have been much easier to cope with difficulties with a teammate. It also would have added more fun to the training process and made it more productive.

The athlete's mood also has a considerable impact on the result. I was alone, so I worked extra with the apparatus at dawn. The group event athletes had just entered the gym, but I had already been waiting for Ireesha. She would come just because of me, and we would start working with two ribbons doing 7-5-4-2 with ankle weights.

Ireesha knew that I would do this plan before the Olympic Games. It was tough to fight exhaustion, pain, and laziness every day. Honestly said, "You are not competing with a rival. You are competing with yourself". The main task is to handle your inner self. I even enjoyed being completely loaded with work. I was proud of my high level of self-consciousness. Even Iryna Deriugina told me, "Why are you doing this? You may just do two or three run-throughs and rest!"

But there in my head was, "Every day, I have to overwork and exhaust myself in the gym. I must be confident enough to go to the Olympic Games." We would do that plan in the morning and the evening. My Mom was there for me during the preparation process, she gave me a lot of support, and I am very grateful to her.

Motivation helped me to endure the most challenging training. The medal in Rio was a dream of my whole life. There was a special place in the gym where I kept a small icon, a picture of a medal, a bag with apparatus, and a Brazilian flag. When I wanted to give up, I looked at the flag, reminding myself what I was suffering for.

In addition, I invented mental training: the last run-through was a mock Olympic performance. Like in a competition, I asked the coaches to invite me to the carpet. I wanted to create the Olympic Games atmosphere around. Later, I also brought my leotards for performances and performed the last repetition wearing them to feel that fear and anxiety. I asked the children to be my loyal audience, creating the necessary mood. I practiced such mock performances every single day. I could perform my routines flawlessly with my eyes closed, and nothing could have spoiled it.

Figure 23. Berlin, 2016. My routine with hoop.

Photo by Ulrich Fabbender

I suffered from some emotional breakdowns before going to Rio, but there were not many of them. Sometimes I wanted to give up, lacking emotional and physical power. I experienced stress, fatigue, and endless competition with myself and everyone around me. During those tough days, I received help from my Mom, Nina, and Ireesha. Having spent four years side by side with the coach, we became close, we were as one, and she knew how to find the right words for me.

There was no need to force me into something. I used to overload myself with work and was very responsible. I just needed someone to help me set myself up emotionally and mentally, not to let me burn out. Ireesha was very good at this.

CHAPTER 39

THE MENTAL ATHLETE

On the verge of my second Olympic Games, I couldn't help thinking about what great athletes of the past felt when they had gone through the same and won their medals. What kind of emotions they felt? Did they have the same fear as me? How did they prepare for the competition? Should I overload myself with work, or should I better to slow down and relax? I wanted to discuss these topics with any of them and ask so many questions.

I watched all kinds of motivational movies I found online: about Muhammad Ali and documentaries about figure skating. It was interesting to know how other athletes overcame difficulties and fear. I have read books like Faster Than Lightning by Usain Bolt and Serve to Win by Novak Djokovic. I wanted to know how to behave before the most important competition of my life. And Ireesha, just a few months before Rio, found me a fantastic book called The Mental Athlete by Kay Porter. It was in English, but we hired a translator. It was a treasure for us.

A psychologist and a coach wrote this book. It is a precise methodological guide on the preparation process of high-performing athletes before the Olympic Games and has to be read by every athlete. In addition, the author gathered data about numerous world celebrities. Kay Porter analyzed people's feelings and fears, suggested ways of coping with them, provided guidance on being ready for extreme situations, and taught how to sharpen your mental skills. It is a non-fiction manual on mental preparation, as athletes usually reach their best physical condition before the

Olympics. But those who manage their inner state get on the Olympic podium.

The Mental Athlete became a guide for me. I even got a diary, where I kept a record of my progress with the help of questions listed in the book. I was physically ready for the competition, but evaluating my mental level was difficult. And this book helped. For instance, I had to answer, "Estimate your inner equilibrium and stress resistance at the moment with points from 1 to 5."

As it appeared, a month before the Olympic Games, my stress resistance was less-than-stellar at three points. I gave four points to my inner strength, self-esteem, and self-confidence. Energy and a strong desire to win were at five points. The answers to such simple questions helped me to see the accurate picture, not to lie to myself, but to understand what I had to work on. The ability to "put up with mistakes" received only two points. I was unable to put up with my mistakes. Negative emotions management was at three points. And after such evaluation, I made a plan for what to do to get five. I made a column called Mental Fortitude Management: Weak Sides.

I had worked on six components: mental preparation, planning for the pre-competition period, mental fortitude, an ability to put up with mistakes, negative thoughts management, and emotional readiness. I was analyzing my mental prep every day. Typically, it is a job of a team therapist, but we didn't have one, so I had to manage my mental health by myself with guidance from Ireesha.

After learning all this new information, I concluded that only positive thinking could help me. Fear was my main enemy. It could simply paralyze me. No matter how well-prepared I was, fear did strike me anyway. There are detailed instructions in the book on how to fight fear. An athlete must be positive, even if anxiety dominates their head. "What if something goes wrong? I lose a club or a ribbon or drop an apparatus? I will not be able to continue my life. I'll jump out of the window!": all these thoughts had to be out.

So here is a dilemma. From one point of view, I had a positive attitude, but on the other hand, I had no idea how to come back home without a medal. For me, it was the end of the world. The stakes were too high. That was how badly I wanted to perform my program without mistakes and win a medal. I wasn't concentrating on the result but on the flawless performance. I had to show my best and no less.

Concentrating on an apparatus and exercise you are doing is another critical skill. It is a common problem when athletes must be more focused in a competition with a big audience. The loss of concentration can lead to severe mistakes. So it is crucial to be present at the moment.

Here are the main aspects of my preparation for the second Olympic Games:

- Positive attitude
- Concentration
- Confidence
- Reaching the best shape before the competition
- Breathing techniques.

I am often asked, "What must we do to eliminate fear?" The secret is to work deeply with yourself. We train our body, but our head also has to be prepared. I remember the last days in Rio before the performance: I was in the middle of the training and suddenly felt paralyzed by fear again; negative thoughts occupied my head. I would go somewhere private, close my eyes, concentrate on a few inspiring phrases, would breathe in and out. I would remind myself all I had known before, "Annie, everything is fine; you are very well prepared, your physical shape is great, you are on the top of your career, and you will be fine." It was my method of setting myself up for positivity and sending negative thoughts away.

One more trick you should remember is breathing; it's an integral part of the preparation process. I took breathing techniques also from the Mental Athlete.

 Fear and anxiety can cause shortness of breath. This shortness of breath symptom can paralyze the body, so there is no chance of performing well. So as soon as I felt fear, which I felt in my stomach,

I started thinking positively, talking to myself, and asking my apparatus to behave and help me. I would breathe in and out a few times. And I felt how the fear faded away.

CHAPTER 40

DOPING

A sensitive topic in the life of every athlete is doping. The all-seeing eye of the World Anti-Doping Agency WADA monitors athletes' "cleanliness." It is an international, independent, non-profit organization leading a worldwide collaborative movement for doping-free sport, composed on behalf of the International Olympic Committee (IOC).

WADA developed the anti-doping system, which is available for every athlete. All prizewinners get into the system automatically and stay under the close supervision of the international anti-doping agency.

Top athletes have their pages in their accounts, which they must fill in with personal information, including location. They have to do so every day, for months, for years. It is obligatory to provide details about nearly every minute of their schedule and inform them about their location in advance for three months. If you go to the competition, you have to tell them about your place of stay and the competition address in advance.

There is a particular column for providing precise information about the location. Filling in the charts caused great inconvenience because all that "writing" distracted me from the most crucial goal. When focusing on the things you are doing, and your main task is to train all day long and perform well, sometimes it is impossible to remember if you filled in the chart.

Sometimes I needed to remember to do it, and a few times, it backfired on me. Usually, the controllers would visit my home to inspect in the morning. Once, I just remembered that I needed to change my location in the chart. Precisely that day, the inspection team came in the evening. I still remember their call, "Anna, where are you? We arrived at your house, but no one opened the door." I answered, "I am at a different location now.

Haven't I stated that in the chart?" In fact, I did not. I wrote that I would be home by 8 p.m. and just went to the supermarket. I had to be fast and come back as soon as possible. They were waiting for me for 15 minutes. Luckily, it ended up well.

Such total control annoyed me because it limited my freedom and rights, making me feel restrained. Someone always watched me. Mentally it was hard. Every move had to be recorded in the personal account. If an athlete gets more than three warnings, it may lead to disqualification. So, I had to remember every step and follow all WADA requirements.

If only you knew how difficult completing all those check-ups during competitions was! World and European championships' award winners, World Cup medalists, and even Grand Prix's prizewinners were all sent to take anti-doping tests.

Sometimes they collected samples for several days. Then, after the final routines, the winners were sent to take doping tests all night long, and the following morning they had to compete in all-around events, which were always very important for everyone. Why all night long? Here is a trick: gymnasts take anti-doping tests very slowly because they drink little water to keep a "cutting" diet. In Rhythmic Gymnastics, weight is more important than health.

After a competition, I usually took a test in a bad mood, realizing I would spend three to four hours in the laboratory. The National Team's doctor was always with me. He had to fill in all the papers. I remember we stayed there until the morning with our doctor Igor Oleksenko. I always failed fast test-taking.

To make it faster, I had to drink water. But extra water meant extra weight and heavy muscles the following day. So, I had to make a choice. Doping control never gave us any pleasure. But, anyway, it is a necessary procedure.

CHAPTER 41

FAREWELL PARTY BEFORE RIO

Traditionally, a year before the Olympic Games and a year after, sports-related events receive significant media coverage. It is sad because people who represent the country internationally lose publicity outside of the Olympic years.

In 2016, before the main competition of the four years, athletes were in the limelight again. It was a great time, and I liked the photo shoots and interviews.

It was apparent to everyone that I could win a medal, so leading newspapers and magazines invited me. I was in photoshoot sessions for Ukrainian Vogue, L'officiel, and Pink. There were a few pages devoted to Ukrainian athletes in every newspaper.

Although these publications distracted me, they helped ease the tension and brought positive emotions. I liked seeing myself on the cover of a famous beauty magazine. However, the coaches didn't fancy the idea of me appearing on the pages of magazines.

Ireesha encouraged my participation in such events, but Iryna Deriugina allowed me to take part in shooting unwillingly. I had to find the right words and proof for a few hours with the press. My appearance in famous publishers helped endorse our sport, so it wasn't just for fun. Iryna Deriugina considered it to be a waste of time. On the contrary, I understood that if I didn't embrace the opportunity, people in Ukraine might have forgotten about Rhythmic Gymnastics.

In 2016, I started working with a manager promoting my name as a brand. Professionals usually spread the athletes' brands from the Western World.

However, in our country, we have to do it by ourselves. I remember in summer, when it was boiling, after exhausting training, I would take a quick shower and apply some make-up; I would rush to a photo shoot or a sporting event. I loved spending time in the company of like-minded people. And back then, there were more than enough different occasions.

On July 11th, there was a presentation of new clothes for the National Team for the 2016 Olympic Games. Andre Tan designed my look and created a uniform for our Olympians in collaboration with the Chinese company Peak. All sports celebrities were invited to the Fashion Show held in Fairmont Grand Hotel. There was a lot of press. I was in a great mood; I loved the bright, pretty, comfortable uniforms. Such events are inspiring; they make you feel that people notice all your efforts.

On July 23rd, the sending-off ceremony to Rio de Janeiro for the National Olympic Team took place in St. Sophia Square. On Saturday evening, hundreds of Kyiv citizens gathered to wish good luck to 205 Olympians in 27 kinds of sports. I was delighted to walk in the front wearing the Olympic uniform with some other athletes and with the Minister of Youth and Sports, Ihor Zhdanov, and the president of NOC, Serhii Bubka.

It was unforgettable! The prime minister of Ukraine, Volodymyr Hroisman, greeted us on Independence Square, Maidan. I memorized his words very well, "Today, you begin your journey to victory." Then Vitalii Kozlovskyi sang the anthem of the Ukrainian National Team. Serhii Bubka, the president of NOC, also made a speech wishing us good luck. I felt people's support, joy, faith, and pride. I saw their smiles and strongly desired not to let them down. In the end, there was a fantastic concert.

I'd also like to share with you one exciting moment right before the Olympics, my birthday. That year on July 16th, I turned 23. As usual, I was in the gym having final training on this day. In this training we used to have every weekend, judges estimated us, and children cheered up. The goal was to make it look like an actual Olympics performance. First, I received congratulations from Albina Deriugina and Iryna Deriugina and then from the girls. Journalists were there to film the training; all in the gym wished me only one thing, to win a medal in Rio. Can you imagine how many words about my victory were there? I strongly felt the unity within our team, and it helped me to complete routines with flying colors.

After I finished, Ireesha sure surprised me. She picked me up in the evening, and we decided to celebrate my birthday in so-called the family circle. There was me, Ireesha, and her husband, Oleksii. We dressed up and went to Gramma, a luxurious restaurant in Kyiv downtown with breathtaking views of the Kyiv Pechersk Lavra and Dnipro. We found a place at the bar right after we entered and waited for Oleksii. Unexpectedly, Ireesha said, "Let's change the location; my husband suggested another place." I was surprised but didn't show it.

When we were leaving the restaurant, two people in hoods attacked us. They appeared out of nowhere. Naturally, I got scared. One of them was holding a knife. They threatened us. I couldn't bear it anymore and screamed.

Eventually, we escaped somehow; wearing high heels, we got to the car and drove away as fast as possible. I kept asking, "Where are we going?" Honestly, I didn't want any celebrations anymore. I had enough adventures for the day. Ireesha tried to calm me down, "It's okay, just some idiots spoiled the mood… Wait for just a little; we are almost there."

Finally, we arrived at the Beach Bora Bora, one of the most spacious places on that side of Dnipro. Ireesha covered my eyes before we entered, and then I saw 15 girls, an amazingly-served table in the open air, and balloons.

It was touching. It was so lovely and unexpected. Finally, Ireesha came to me and confessed that the attack was just a prank. We laughed at it together. Ultimately, we had a big cake decorated with

Olympic rings and a medal with the signature "Rio." What was my birthday wish? You guess!

CHAPTER 42

READY AND WILLING

The Olympic preparations were almost over. And it was a relief. On my way to Brazil, I felt fulfilled and had done my best. The coaching staff decided to come to Brazil earlier to have enough time for acclimatization to cope with jet lag. The pre-Olympic period took us ten days. During that time, we were staying in a hotel in Vitoria city. We had access to the fantastic gym with two standard carpets. In Ukraine, we didn't have such luxury.

Iryna Deriugina led daily warm-ups. There was no 7-5-4-2 plan this time. The most challenging part was already over. Muhammad Ali once said, "The fight is won or lost far away from the witnesses, behind the lines, in the gym and out there on the road, long before I dance under those lights." That is so true. I felt it myself.

In Brazil, we got the second wind. Nobody felt any tiredness or pain. There needed to be more sense in learning something new. We had another task: to cope with all the mental tension, strengthen all we knew, brush up on it, and keep it until the Olympic Games. My daily plan was to do three flawless run-throughs of every routine in the morning and evening. All went well. I felt I was ready like never before.

The coaches and the judge of Ukraine's National rhythmic gymnastics team, Yuliia Antrushkevych, were helping us. We have become very close with Yuliia in the last four years. She had been evaluating all my performances. So we had a common goal, and it cheered me up. I felt how all around were supporting us and how they worried about our performances. But sometimes, gymnasts could lose their temper due to rising tension and require a delicate approach. Otherwise, girls could "sting" them back. Fortunately, I was treated very well by Ireesha, Iryna Deriugina, and Yuliia Antrushkevych. There were no arguments, only support.

Natália Gaudio, the first number on the Brazilian National team, trained at the same gym. When we finished, her training session started. Once, she brought the Olympic torch to the gym. It inspired me. We held it for some time, took pictures, and made a wish.

In Vitoria, two testing training were held with spectators cheering for us. The atmosphere was so lovely and cheerful that I had no reason to get nervous. I would come to the carpet and do routine repetitions even with my eyes shut.

Such warm displays of support deeply touched my heart. Then, one day, Ireesha brought Brazilian acai ice cream to raise my spirits. I liked it because it was a heavenly delight for sweet tooths with coconut water. Sometimes, happiness comes from simple things.

But also, we had to follow some strict rules. Before the Olympic Games, the coaches wanted to take our phones away to protect us from some external factors and irritation and not to let us read comments and different points of sports analysts. Everyone knew how it could influence me. But I won my smartphone back after convincing them I needed to keep in touch with my parents badly. So I got it back but promised I would not read news about myself.

In ten days, our team moved to Rio. We all smiled, leaving the airport. Firstly, an exhausting preparation process was over, and it made us happy. Secondly, we saw Brazil as a sunny country with positive vibes everywhere. After seeing Rio, the sun, and the smiles on people's faces, we immediately felt the extraordinary beauty of life. When we arrived at the Olympic Village, I felt joy.

The vibe in the city where the most renowned athletes from all over the world gathered was fabulous. I was so proud to be there. We were so close to the moment X. I knew rehearsals were over; I just had to show up on the carpet and do it.

We lived in the same block with the coaches and group performers. Iryna Deriugina was living separately in the hotel. Ireesha and the National Team's doctor Igor Oleksenko kept eyeing me. Igor even accompanied me to the Olympic canteen. I wasn't left alone at all. All cared about me and protected me.

Because we didn't have a team therapist, Ireesha and our doctor replaced the one for me, they were like titanium for me, not letting me lose faith. I could share all I was anxious about and discuss how I felt. It was the fourth Olympics for Igor, and his experience was tremendous. Every evening athletes came to get a piece of advice from him. I would pretend I needed some treatment but just needed to talk.

I had to share emotions, fears, and doubts with somebody. We were spending enough time with Igor, and he could recognize my condition very fast. He told me a few days before the start, "You are doing fine. The most important - no emotional swings, don't wind yourself up, don't overthink, never doubt your chances to win." I memorized those words well.

From the very first days in Rio, we were doing our best. And then, there was the first training session in the arena. I finally saw gymnasts from other countries gathered together. It was crucial to present myself properly, to show what I could do. Everybody was tense: no smiles or minimum contact. Everyone focused only on themselves.

The journalists were already there to film all the training. I didn't even know who those people were. After the exercise, they interviewed me. They turned out to be Korean reporters. They asked me one provoking question, "You probably realize if you want to reach the podium, you must exceed a Korean gymnast Son Yeon-jae. So what are you going to do?"

I don't remember what I replied, but I knew that the competition would be hot, because every girl craved so badly to win, but there couldn't be only three winners. A considerable drawback of our type of sport is the need for finals; they are only all-around. All athletes were in their best physical shape so that they would fight to the bitter end; everyone deserves to win.

Then training on the stage began, and we saw the hall where we would perform. I did everything okay. There were judges present. This stage requires one to be confident and function well. The coaches used to tell us, "The way you perform in the final rehearsal, the same way your main performance will look like." The judges pay attention and mark who and how they perform. They checked our readiness.

I remember bright lights. Our carpet was on the platform. It was unusual; we performed above judges and coaches. Even though the light was dazzling, I effectively showed myself and checked how the apparatus worked. The rehearsal was successful. After this, I became more confident.

We took part in a Gala concert before the competition. It was a great chance to try the main stage. So we got an extra opportunity to feel the Olympic vibe.

There is no secret that rhythmic gymnasts perform at the end of the Olympics. Usually, when all other athletes have finished and can walk around with beaming smiles, rhythmic gymnasts only start fighting. So this is a challenge. But there was also a perk: other athletes were cheering for us.

CHAPTER 43

QUALIFICATION

The day of the performance was coming. I moved in with a group events gymnast Yevgeniya Gomon. We got on well with her. Yevgeniya used to live with me in my flat some time ago, so there was no discomfort this time. Moreover, we met only before going to bed. Our training schedules were so hectic that we had no energy and time for conversations at the end of the day. So when we met in the evening, we usually asked each "How is it going?" and that was it.

I want to devote a separate paragraph to our preparation with Ireesha in Rio. I am a person who has got my rituals. Emotional stamina before the performance is an essential thing for me. In the evening, I would pray. Before going to bed, I would conduct autogenic training: I would close my eyes and imagine myself doing the program flawlessly.

In the morning, my mood would depend on how well my make-up was or how well I combed my hair. If I managed to do everything correctly from the first attempt, I would feel calm and relaxed. The day has begun well; everything is going to be okay. But if I failed my make-up routine or couldn't manage my hair, I would be immediately struck, thinking that something might go wrong.

Music helped me to set the mood. On the way from the Olympic Village to the arena, I listened to my favorite songs by Lana Del Rey and Michael Jackson. It was my escape from negative thoughts, always trying to get into my head and distracting me from vital tasks. I would wear ankle weights with earphones in my ears for a warm-up.

Every morning I received a video message from Ireesha, in which she called me a tiny cute diamond. So, the first thing I would hear in the morning would be, "Good morning, tiny diamond! It is your day! Shine bright! I'm looking forward to seeing you in the gym!" I like those videos.

During the training, we finished each other's sentences. Ireesha felt me. As soon as I started to warm up, she would recognize my physical and mental state and mood and use accurate, fitting words to hit a target. She was always smiling, trying to convey only positive emotions to me. It helped tremendously.

We were very open to each other. If I got scared, I could come to Ireesha and share; she helped me overcome this. One more important moment for me, I never allowed anyone except Ireesha to help me to get dressed before competing. I would always zip my leotard up or let Ireesha do it. She was the only person I trusted completely.

The Ukrainian gymnast Oleg Verniaiev came to our room the day before qualification to see us. By that time, he had already become an Olympic champion. He let us hold his Olympic medal for some time. It was inspiring for everyone, and we made wishes. Finally, after having prayed, I fell asleep.

The qualification day came. Surprisingly, I was in a great mood. I knew we would wait to fight for medals, and there was some space for a mistake. The main task was to get into the top 10. I was sure I would get into the top 10 without serious mistakes. And that happened.

Due to the Olympic Games' rules, gymnasts can be accompanied to the performance area only by one coach. I was worried about who it would be. When competition organizers said that only one coach had to stay, Albina and Iryna Deriuginas arose from the chairs and went to the stands. Both of them realized, for me, it was easier emotionally to be accompanied by Ireesha. A doctor or a massage therapist was also allowed to be there, so we had Igor Oleksenko by our side. Now, I can't even imagine how nervous Ireesha was, accompanying me to a competition of such a level. She was early in her career, so it was a huge responsibility.

Qualification performances took the whole day; we competed for over eight hours. There were two hours breaks. We had never performed at such a slow pace, so it was odd. Luckily, we had been aware of this and followed the same speed in training: doing one routine – two hours for a break, then the second routine and a break. This schedule was opposite from what I liked. My muscles were "getting cold"; before starting the following exercise, I had to warm up again four times. But, before the Olympic Games, we had nailed all ins and outs.

The endless day took everything out of me. I just wanted to finish. But, having inside that feeling of readiness, I understood that I had to save energy because the following day would be the most important. The audience was cheering for me. While doing my ribbon samba routine, all spectators seemed to be standing next to me on the carpet.

All ended in eight hours. Luckily, it ended up victorious for me. I performed without mistakes. The only strange thing that happened to me when I lost a toe shoe doing a hoop routine. It feels odd to continue a performance when your toe shoe is in the middle of the carpet. And you know where the funniest part begins? The first thought I had was, "Is my pedicure okay?" The whole world was watching my toes.

I became the third. When the qualification competition ended, I thought, "God, why weren't we competing for medals?" I did well with all routines; I was calm and confident. Perfect mood to be! After the competition, Serhii Bubka came to see Ireesha and me. He had the experience of being a FIG judge, sitting at the same table as Bruno Grandi, the president of the FIG. He knew a thing or two about disagreements that may arise between judges in our type of sport. Serhii Bubka decided to back up our rhythmic gymnastics team personally. Coming to the carpet, I found him with my eyes. Seeing a familiar person at the FIG judge's table helped me to concentrate.

Leaving the performance area and finally being able to "switch myself off," I noticed a Ukrainian stand with a passionate audience. It felt so good to see other Ukrainian winners: Zhan Beleniuk, who had won the silver medal in Rio; Olha Kharlan, a Ukrainian fencer, the Olympic champion in 2008; Olena Hovorova, the bronze medal winner of the Olympics in Sidney.

Such moments taught me that we all are one big Ukrainian sports family. My heart was full of gratitude for the fact that so many athletes were supporting me. I still remember the words Serhii Bubka told me that day, "The main thing you have to do tomorrow is not to exceed yourself. There is no need for something new, do just the same thing you did today, with tranquility, do all you know." Receiving a piece of advice from a legendary athlete was something I needed at that moment. Then I started to prepare myself for the following day mentally.

CHAPTER 44

THE MOMENT OF TRUTH

When I opened my eyes in the morning, I felt a tiny lump of fear squirming inside my stomach. The day I had been waiting for so long finally came! I suddenly felt the urge to escape; I wanted to hide somewhere from this burden of responsibility and wait for the unknown. I had been preparing so hard, having gone through a lot to receive the second Olympic license, and after all this, I was still frightened!

I put on my clothes, styled my hair, applied make-up, and went to the canteen. Igor and Ireesha were already there. I discussed my mood with Igor during breakfast and went to warm up. I had to be ready for the performance physically and mentally. I knew I had to be brave and put all my doubts aside. I was more prepared than ever.

There were tons of disturbing thoughts whirling in my head. I tried hard to send them away. During a two-hour-long warm-up, I looked insane talking to myself. I tried to set my brain up for positive vibes. However, the competitive spirit was already flying in the air and was hard to ignore. A fiery competitive feeling was growing every minute. I was changing before the performance, realizing it was about 20 minutes before the start. I couldn't stop thinking, "What will happen now?!"

The second competition day was completely different. It was even more frightening and nerve-wracking. I realized I had a chance only that day because there were no finals in Rhythmic Gymnastics. Mentally it was hard to bear. I also wanted to know whether Serhii Bubka would be present during our performances, as it was the last day of the Olympic Games and the last chance for the Ukrainian

National Team to win. Walking to the carpet, I saw him, and it comforted me.

The first performance was with a hoop, which was supposed to be my best. I made no serious mistakes, but it could have been better too. I looked more confident the day before, performing a qualification hoop routine. Having finished the first type, I reached fourth place. Sitting in the Kiss and Cry zone with Ireesha, I realized hundreds of run-throughs were for nothing, and my medal was slipping out of my hands. It is a challenging task to catch up on the points you lost in our type of sport. There were three complicated routines I was about to perform.

It is hard to describe what I felt at that moment! It was indeed a turning point, my moment of truth. The crucial task was to manage my emotions. It was the end: the time to pack suitcases, go home and kill myself. And all this because I didn't do my best routine flawlessly, which I could do with my eyes closed! I got an average score for my first performance. Ireesha hugged me, but I was angry myself.

Everyone on my team became nervous. Iryna Deriugina, who was staying in the stands, called Ireesha. Ireesha also got worried, knowing how much responsibility she had. The primary coaches already barely could stand our collaboration. So, how much mudslinging would be there if we didn't meet their expectations? She was straightforward, saying, "Enough, let's do more run-throughs. Now!"

No one did that. All gymnasts were so prepared that they only practiced their essential elements and went on stage. But, Ireesha told me to run the routines. And I did everything flawlessly; everything ran like clockwork. Then, having repeated my routines three times each, I burst into tears. I felt so resented, "Gosh, I am so prepared! But it's the fear that's stopping me. Will I give up because of a strange feeling? Will I give my dream to someone else?"

I got furious. At that moment, Igor Oleksenko came to me and said just one phrase, "Just go and do it! Show them that you've got Tatar blood in your veins!" It was an inside joke we had. He used to call me Tatar, referring to my Crimean Tatar heritage. But this time, his words touched my heart. The blood of my ancestors started to rage inside me.

Performing a ball routine, I was in a completely different mood. It looked like an alien, a much weaker version of me, performed a hoop routine earlier. I concentrated on the ball routine, like iron: no emotions or personal feelings. First, I had to appear and take off, jumping from fifth place to first. In that case, I would catch up. Doing everything just good wasn't enough. I had to be excellent to reach the podium, nail all elements, and perform well.

By watching the Olympics video, one may notice that even my walk changed: this time, I was strolling; I needed to feel every step. I started to breathe correctly, concentrated on myself, and balanced everything to the maximum. I mentally isolated myself from the outer world; I didn't hear noise from the stands nor see judges. There was only me and my ball. I realized I would get a chance if I did a ball routine well. All my sports career was at stake.

I remember all: how music started to play, my movements, the ball in the air. Then, in a split second, the audience burst into cheers. It was magical; I felt connected to everyone in the crowd. Indescribable feeling! I did a ball routine with flying colors! When I caught the ball for the last time, I breathed out and sighed, "Good Lord! I did it!"

I felt I could still win. I did what I had to do, and I succeeded! I got more points from the judges. Having finished a ball routine, I was in third place. And even though I felt thrilled inside, my face was cold as ice. It was too early to celebrate; I was about to do two more routines. When I arrived at Kiss and Cry zone, I immediately started concentrating on upcoming clubs, "There are two clubs, and I have to watch them. My hands are sweaty, so I must watch out not to drop them."

Having changed a leotard for a club's routine, I did a few repetitions to the music. I felt the vibe and achieved just the right emotional state. As a result, I performed my club's routine excellently. However, I was overly concerned about balance. When

I was standing on one foot and the other foot, which shook a little bit, was holding a club, there came some dreadful thoughts, "What if a club won't fly in the right direction? How will I continue, then? If I lose a club, there won't be any hope." In my experience, delivering a baby is easier than conquering the tension of competing for a medal.

After it went well initially, and I felt how a club got into my hand after the first foot movement, I kept doing the routine with growing confidence. I was doing the event to the music of my favorite, Michael Jackson, almost like a robot. It was accurate and precise. I couldn't show my emotions then. The main task was to focus on the apparatus, not drop it, to complete every movement. As a professional gymnast, I was following a checking card. My mission was complete; however, I was still third. Ireesha still appeared anxious, but I was calmer than ever.

I was getting ready for a ribbon event. I begged, "Dear God, don't let silly things happen like a knot on my ribbon!" I was terrified of unexpected things. It could be the most frustrating experience.

In the training zone, I worked alongside Russian gymnast Yana Kudryavtseva. We were not watching other girls' performances; we tried to focus only on ourselves. Then, suddenly, I looked at the screen with the results. I noticed a Belarusian gymnast Melitina Stanyuta with the head coach of the Belarusian National team Irina Leparskaya. She was weeping on the coach's shoulder, who was crying as well. Although we were rivals with Melitina, I felt terrible for her. Seeing the disappointment on her face, I understood her dream hadn't come true. There was nothing she could do about that. She had to move on.

It was my biggest fear. I felt a lump in my throat. I was trying my best to perform a ribbon routine, praying and trying so hard that I probably looked possessed. It would have been unbearable to start the final type being third and end up beyond the podium.

Walking to the carpet, I didn't see anyone or hear anything. My focus was on the ribbon. A ribbon is the most complicated apparatus, which is easy to blow away or lose in the projector's blinds. Having completed the first part of the event, where I had the riskiest elements, I whispered to myself, "Be careful, pay attention to details, and move a wrist in a position to feel the stick. Good! Well done!" Thirty seconds before the

Figure 24. The Olympics in Rio, 2016. Ireesha and I are crying after my final routine

end of the routine, when all tricky elements were finished, there was only a pirouette and a dance step combination left; I relaxed and performed it with great artistic expression. My mood immediately changed. I showed all I could. The game was over.

Figure 25. The Olympic Podium. Margarita Mamun (Gold), Yana Kudryavtseva (Silver), Anna Rizatdinova (Bronze).

Photo by NOC Ukraine

Many people thought I was crying because I took only third place. No! I wept for joy because I managed to do it, and everything finally ended. It was a relief. I was walking and realized what was happening: I heard crowd cheers and voices from Ukrainian stands, saw faces, and felt immense happiness. I ran to Ireesha, flung myself into her arms, and cried because everything had ended!

It was what I was dreaming about! I had been moving towards this moment for so many years, had been thinking about this, imagining. It came true. There is a number three on the screen next to my name. We've got the medal!

Figure 26. Happy End of the Olympics!

Nina Yeresko was the first to call my Mom from the stands and tell her delightful news. Mom was at St Petro and Pavlo Cathedral in Simferopol. Ireesha was over the moon, but I had no energy to express my emotions. My dream came true! My journey from Crimea to Olympic Bronze was finally over!

Figure 27. Winning my Bronze Medal. The moment of truth.

Photo by NOC Ukraine

THANKS FOR READING

After reading my memoirs, I hope you will find inspiration and wisdom to continue doing what you do, even if your life has nothing to do with sports. I appreciate your support in the uneasy journey of writing this book. I wouldn't be who I am without you.

Do you want to be in touch?

I will gladly answer your letters sent to this email: fromcrimeatobronze@gmail.com

ABOUT THE AUTHOR

Anna Rizatdinova is a Ukrainian Rhythmic Gymnast, the bronze medalist of the Olympic Games in Rio de Janeiro in 2016, the world champion with the hoop in 2013, a multi-award winner of the world championships of Europe and of the summer Universiades, the merited master of sports of Ukraine, the holder of the order of Princess Olga of I and II degrees.

Her way to the top of the elite athlete status was like a bed of thorns. She faced great career take-offs, bitter disappointments, doubts, and everyday hard work. And now, having gone through a challenging but fascinating journey, she wants to share all tricks and secrets of her favorite sport.

Printed in Great Britain
by Amazon

25442443R00116